WITHIN
These Borders

) Spanish-Speaking Peoples in the U.S.A. (

WITHIN
These Borders

by JOHN R. SCOTFORD

FRIENDSHIP PRESS — NEW YORK

LIBRARY OF CONGRESS CATALOG CARD NUMBER: 53-9345

To you, my Mexican and Puerto Rican friends, in the hope that this volume may lead others to enjoy you as much as I have

Contents

Foreword

The following pages provide only glimpses of a notable part of the population of the United States. No matter how expert and sensitive the reporter nor how large the book, one treatment cannot possibly do justice to Spanish Americans. There are a million of them in Texas, 760,000 in California, 250,000 in New Mexico, 25,000 in both Arizona and Colorado, 37,000 in New York, plus a scattered half million of illegal entrants. Add to these the Cubans in Tampa and visiting students from every Latin American country. Such figures merely illustrate the weakness of arithmetic to bring a sense of reality to the description of a people.

Something of Spanish culture and its contributions to life in the United States is found in these pages. But again, describing Spanish art, music, and architecture fails to reveal to the remote reader the warmth and vitality of the people. Surveys might tabulate the exact number of Spanish Protestant Christians, the number of ministers who

serve them, and the value in dollars of their churches. Such information would serve only to overload the brain without producing a
clarifying vision.

To appreciate any people one must communicate with them per-
sonally and so arrive at an understanding derived from experience.
Without such personal contact, the best we can do is to feel vicariously
the attitudes of those who do know them. Such are the Christian
workers who for Christ's sake have devoted their lives to sharing the
fruit of the gospel with them.

A characteristic common to those who are in "Spanish-speaking
work" is a vibrant enthusiasm for their parishioners and co-workers.
This grows from an appreciation of the values that develop in the
soul when Christ has wrought his gracious change. If those workers
could speak to us in our churches they would strive above all else to
communicate to us their own radiant enthusiasm. "Here are people
for whom Christ died," they would say. "These are our brothers re-
deemed, living new, victorious lives in him." Are we their keepers?
The answer surely is "No! We are called by Christ to be their brothers."

These pages also show examples of Christian work in evangelism
and education and social service. How may we see the full Christian
program throughout the states and so appreciate its importance? The
visiting missionary can make us respond to his conviction of a great
missionary opportunity. The majority of Americans of Spanish heritage
know Christianity only in a cultural sense. Without an effective ministry they have resorted to superstition, but their response to Christian
love is both ready and profound.

Missionaries have a harvest to show for the planting. Their stories
tell of broken lives made new, immoral people made holy, and untaught
children brought to glad graduation. Behold the little cotton picker
now a Christian nurse. Hear of the staunch elder whose back still

bears a cross of scars inflicted by the whips of the Penitente orgy. Wonder at the bandit who once rode with Pancho Villa, now, by God's grace, a Christian pastor. Theirs are dramatic, moving stories and necessarily so, for how can miracles be reported in cold blood?

Within the limits imposed by modesty, the missionary could portray the Christian program as being good—as good as resources of leadership and equipment will allow. True enough, many chapels and churches are humble, since the little congregations are poor. But supporting friends can do a great deal to make these centers of worship and education more nearly adequate. Surely we will not blame the missionaries for conditions caused by weak support.

It is also true that many Spanish pastors need more and better training. This lack, however, need be no reflection upon their devotion nor upon their ability to evoke from their people a fervent allegiance. There is plenty of room for both pastors and people to grow, and they hope to occupy additional space.

Christian workers among Spanish people in the United States believe the field is ready for harvest and appeal for more workers to do the reaping. They hope that God will raise us up to become wholehearted participants in the redemptive endeavor that is their lifework. Their supreme trust is in the Lord of the harvest.

Hardheaded citizens may ask what practical good comes from Protestant mission work. Some may be comforted with school and hospital statistics, others with success stories of people helped to "make good." Christian workers, though, would prefer to speak of the needs felt by citizens of Spanish culture and point to the values they themselves discover in Christian experience.

Although Spanish people may be locally numerous in some places, nationally they are a minority. Like other minorities they need friendship in a new land. Where better can friendship be found than in

Christ and in the fellowship of his people? Spanish Christians know how to return friendship in unstinted measure, for they are poets at heart. Spanish friendship, however, is so tinctured with courtesy that it may tax the sense of efficiency of some North Americans.

Another need felt by a minority group is for justice—a fair chance to make a living and build a life. This does not mean asking favors, for Spanish citizens accept heavy duties that the average North American would refuse to bear. A young Puerto Rican mother raising four little ones in a Brooklyn apartment works all day in a candy factory, prepares the next day's meals at night, and shows the eldest daughter how to care for the younger ones until her return in the late afternoon. When asked if she found this life difficult, she replied in surprise, "But no. It is my work. Why should I think it hard?" This mother keeps the apartment and tries to keep up with her children's interests. She asks for work at a fair wage and a chance for the children to grow. May she expect her church to be a champion of justice?

Minorities are like majorities in one respect; all the people who comprise them need a Saviour. Surely the yearning love of God demonstrated in the world mission of the church seeks to embrace Spanish-speaking Americans.

A teen-age Puerto Rican boy in Brooklyn was one among eight school children recognized for outstanding citizenship. Though he had been in the United States only three years, he had become his teacher's interpreter. In answer to a letter from a mission board secretary he replied, "You encourage me to go ahead by the Golden Rule. I say I do, I will, I promise, not only to you, or to my parents or teachers, but to myself and my God. You also want to know from where did I learn the Golden Rule. I'll answer, from my mother, from my teachers, from the ministers of God. Who knows? I'm sure all of them had planted a little bit on my soul."

Many Spanish Americans with cultivated souls are contributing increasingly to the richness of life in the United States. Some have taken places of top leadership in business and politics. Increasingly they are found as professors in colleges and universities. In the realm of drama consider such names as José Ferrer, Diosa Costella, Olga San Juan, and Juano Hernandez. In music few stars shine brighter than pianist Jesús María Sanroma, composer and orchestra leader Noro Morales, and the coloratura soprano of the Metropolitan Opera, Graciela Rivera. Many other areas of endeavor find Spanish names among the leaders, including major league baseball, with Ruben Gomez pitching for the New York Giants. Will anyone blame the missionary for believing that what a few have already done, large numbers will do in the future by God's grace?

A graduate student in New York University came from humble circumstances in Puerto Rico. She had no money nor influential friends as a young girl, but she made the most of real ability and a burning ambition to learn. A mission college in the United States offered her a chance to earn a higher education.

Recently she appeared before a church audience to tell her experience. Those present saw a vivacious young miss, head tied in a silk scarf with saucy ends lying on her left shoulder, step to the speaker's stand. Sensing the kindness of the Christian friends before her, she discarded her notes, and told eloquently of her life.

"How real! How refreshing!" her listeners commented. They were captivated by her natural exuberance as she spoke with unfeigned gratitude of her development as a child of their common Saviour.

All of us in North America need that Spanish exuberance of spirit. Christians of Spanish culture may well bring such refreshment to American Christendom.

LESLIE C. SAYRE

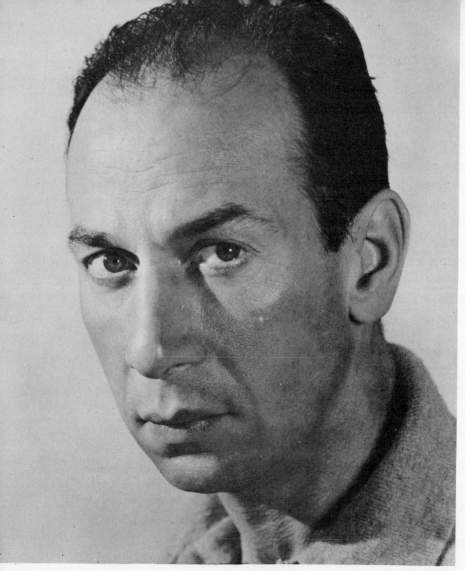

José Ferrer, brilliant actor-director. He holds honorary degrees from Princeton and the University of Puerto Rico.

) CHAPTER 1 (

Spanish—But Not from Spain

AMONG the four or five million Spanish-speaking Americans are the descendants of some of the oldest settlers within our boundaries and also the newest arrivals on the shores of continental United States.

At one extreme are the Old Spanish who have been living in the remote valleys of New Mexico for nearly three and a half centuries; at the other are the plane loads of Puerto Ricans who drop down out of the air to throng the streets of New York city. Other old-timers are the descendants of the original settlers of California, Texas, and Florida—a very select and hard to identify company. Other newcomers are the Mexicans who have been swarming back and forth across our southern border for the past half century.

The composition of these groups is varied. The earliest settlers probably had the purest Spanish blood, but three to four centuries away from Spain have brought an inevitable dilution. The Spaniards conquered the Indians of Mexico, and then the Indians absorbed the Spaniards. In Puerto Rico three principal strains have mingled: Spanish, Indian, and Negro, and in the process the Indian elements have disappeared. The Spanish strain appears to be dominant, but it is far removed from Spain and much mingled with the other two.

The tie that binds Spanish-speaking Americans together is the culture that the conquering Spaniard bestowed upon them, not blood. In many ways these intrepid sons of Spain were remarkable teachers. They are dead, but their language, their culture, and their religion flourish in most of the New World.

The attitude of the Spanish-speaking peoples of the Americas toward Spain is most curious. They have no apparent interest in Spain. Their lines of travel run to Paris and New York rather than Madrid. Mexicans, Puerto Ricans, and the other peoples of Central and South America use the means of communication and the ways of life that the Spaniards taught them, and yet are in no sense Spanish themselves.

This lack of attachment shows particularly in their attitude toward their language. Spanish is a great tongue. It has rare beauty. It is the most logical of languages. It is rich in humor. Yet the millions in America who use it seem to regard it primarily as a convenience. The children of Spanish-speaking parents are so eager to learn English in their new homeland that they are loathe to admit that they even understand Spanish. The writer has repeatedly tried to engage boys and girls of Mexican descent in conversation in Spanish, but his usual reward is a frown. The Spanish language is a flimsy barrier to Americanization. This is unfortunate. Spanish culture deserves to be preserved.

Individualism is one of the striking aspects of Spanish culture. This is well described by President Samuel Nelson of the Spanish American Baptist Seminary in Los Angeles: "The typical Spanish American tends to be individualistic and to think in terms of personality rather than organization. Loyalty to country has never been to the Latin American as significant as the attraction of a strong individual leader. At best this trait manifests itself in a larger concern for the interests and ideals of humanity than for loyalty to an institution or to the state. It has its disadvantage in making it difficult at times for.him to cede personal interests and sovereignty for the welfare of the group."[1] This individualism makes for personal touchiness and has a connection with the lack of strong social and other organizations among Spanish-speaking people. Their interests center in the home. And yet their individualism is not as ingrained as it appears. Labor unions have had considerable success among Mexicans, while the Puerto Ricans of New York city are among the most loyal supporters of the garment trades' and hotel workers' organizations. To quote a Denver observer again, "Mexicans will not organize just for the sake of an organization, as Americans often do. They must have a strong purpose before they will combine their efforts. Given that and they work together splendidly!"

This same trait is found in their attitude toward the Roman Catholic Church. They are in it but not a part of it. Here again we will quote President Samuel Nelson: "Of little significance for 90 per cent of the Spanish American people as a faith to live by, it still forms the foundation of their culture. While the faith of Roman Catholicism has never in reality possessed the Spanish heart, as a social and cultural framework its control has been tremendous. Historically its genius has been adaptation. Among Spanish-speaking peoples it has adapted itself to their individualistic and independent temper by permitting each man to possess his own heart while controlling his mind and way of life through the mysterious beauty of its sacraments and its material power."

[1] The quotations from President Nelson are from an article to be published by the American Baptist Home Missionary Society. Used by permission.

The Roman Catholic Church has a remarkable talent for appealing to the imagination of its people without laying too great a burden upon their will. In Mexico the church buildings are always dramatic, even though they may lack much in the way of beauty. They are often in striking contrast to the homes of the people. The appeal is to the heart rather than to the head.

Neither the Mexicans nor the Puerto Ricans have brought the Roman Catholic Church with them in the way that other immigrant groups have done. In the mill towns of New England one will often find an Irish, a French, and a Polish Roman Catholic church, each standing as a monument to the devotion of an immigrant group, and each served by priests of the appropriate nationality. Spanish-speaking immigrants have not followed this pattern at all. There are six Spanish Roman Catholic churches in New York city, but they are run by monastic orders for Spaniards from Spain and have little to do with the thousands of supposed Roman Catholics who are pouring in from Puerto Rico.

As far as we have been able to discover, there are no Roman Catholic churches in this country that have been built by immigrants from Mexico or Puerto Rico. A rather typical situation is that in Detroit, where a church that was built by Irish immigrants sixty or seventy years ago now serves a colony from the Isle of Man and a group of Mexicans and Puerto Rican newcomers under the leadership of an Irish priest. Here the policy of the diocese is to speed assimilation by having new national groups move in with established parishes. This has some advantages, but it is not conducive to making the newcomer in a new land feel at home.

In its ministries to Spanish-speaking Americans the Roman Catholic Church suffers from two handicaps.

The first is the poverty of the newcomers. They have the poorest paying jobs, they live in the least desirable neighborhoods, and they have little money for church support. This is aggravated by the fact that they had had no training in systematic church support in the places whence they came. The usual pattern in the Roman Catholic Church is for each parish to pay its own way, with the priest looking to his parishioners for support. This has often been impossible with the newly arrived Mexicans and Puerto Ricans. Such a situation can be met in two ways. One is to bring additional revenue into a parish by making it a shrine. This has been done with the two churches in Chicago that avowedly minister to Mexicans. The other procedure is to turn a parish over to a monastic order, which is able to supplement the parish revenues. This has been done in a number of instances in New York city.

The second and greater source of weakness of the Roman Catholic Church is the lack of Puerto Rican and Mexican priests. As a sacerdotal church it judges its success by the measure in which it makes the sacraments available to the people. The priest stands at the center of the Roman Catholic religion. We have already mentioned how the loyalties of those trained in the Spanish tradition are personal rather than institutional. Mexicans and Puerto Ricans will go to both confession and the altar with much more willingness if the priest to whom they go is one of their own people. Yet there are no Puerto Rican priests and few if any Mexican ones in this country! Probably the reason for this is that there are very few vocations for the priesthood in either country. According to John Considine, in *Call for Forty Thousand*,[2] it would take 40,000 additional priests to supply the people living south of the Rio Grande with the same sort of ministry to which the Roman Catholics of the United States are accustomed.

The Mexican or Puerto Rican coming to the United States to live is exposed to two contradictory impulses. As a stranger in a strange

[2] New York, Longmans, Green and Co., 1946.

land there is the natural tendency to cling to that which is old and familiar. Our land is dotted with language churches built by the immigrants of previous years. Over against this is the impulse to follow the dictum "when in Rome do as the Romans do." The breaking of old social and cultural ties may make it easier to break religious ties as well.

Apparently the Mexicans are more inclined to cling to the old and the Puerto Ricans to conform to the new—at least it is reported that the Puerto Ricans are more receptive to Protestantism in New York than they are at home. We suspect that this goes back to two other things. In Mexico the Roman Catholic Church was purged by persecution under the Calles regime and in recent years has been enjoying a spiritual renaissance that is being felt to some extent north of the border, while under the American flag the Roman Catholic Church in Puerto Rico has been neither harassed nor helped but has had to stand on its own. Also the transition that the Mexican experiences in crossing the Rio Grande is not nearly so dramatic as that which befalls the Puerto Rican when he flies from San Juan to New York city. The change in total environment may make the latter a bit more willing to shift his religious allegiance.

Where does Protestantism fit into this picture?

In some ways it is the reverse of Roman Catholicism. It lacks the imposing framework of massive buildings, institutions, and ecclesiastical officials. It does not shape the culture of Spanish-speaking lands. On the other hand, at its best it speaks with power to the heart of the individual. It lacks the support of "everybody is doing it," and yet it has transforming power over human life.

Protestantism is not alien to the Spanish way of life. It is not something that is solely associated with the Anglo-Americans. Even in Spain there are Protestants who are holding to their faith in the face of persecution. In Mexico the total Protestant community includes between 250,000 and 400,000 people. Many individual Protestants are widely respected. In Puerto Rico Protestantism has penetrated into every corner of the island, and leadership is being assumed by the Puerto Ricans themselves. Protestantism is not something bearing the brand "Made in the United States."

In striking contrast to the Roman Catholic Church, Protestantism has been able to produce an indigenous leadership for its churches. It is quite unusual for an American to serve as pastor of a Spanish-speaking church; most of the ministers share the life and background of their congregations. This makes for understanding and sincere friendliness. It is a priceless asset.

The individual looms large in Protestantism. All souls are important in the eyes of God, and every man, woman, and child has significance in the life of a congregation. This builds self-respect, which is greatly needed by most newcomers to our land. Even though one is poor and pushed about, he becomes aware that he is a son of God when he enters a Protestant church.

But these advantages are simply the foreshadowing of the fundamental truth of Protestantism, that we have the right of free access to our Heavenly Father through Jesus Christ. Ours is a personal faith in a personal God. This has a strong appeal to Spanish Americans, only they do not respond in the same way as Anglo-Americans. As President Nelson puts it, "While many are won to Christ in the Spanish American churches their membership remains small. The typical Anglo-American can scarcely conceive of his faith apart from the institution that sustains it and gives it expression. Many a Spanish American sees little point in joining an organization when his needs are so fully satisfied by a personal faith in Christ as Saviour and Lord. The eagerness with which he responds to the appeal of Christ is so great as to be almost pathetic. But to make a public stand means breaking with his culture, cutting social and often family relationships, and in many ways making a radical change in his way of life. This requires great faith and more courage than many of us would possess. Only with difficulty is the Spanish American of Catholic background brought to the place of being an active, baptized member of an evangelical church."

Its practical helpfulness is one aspect of Protestantism that is greatly appreciated by Spanish-speaking Americans. Nearly all feel themselves to be strangers in a strange land. They are naturally suspicious of an environment that they do not fully understand. Problems of all sorts confront them: difficulties with the law, troubles in business, and matters of ill health. Their great need is for an understanding friend. This is the role of the Protestant pastor and of the workers in the Homes of Friendly Service that are maintained by home mission agencies in many communities—and under a variety of names.

Protestant helpfulness is usually related to the practical needs. of the people. When the foods to which one has been accustomed are hard to get, and when the stove is a very different contraption from what one had back in Zamora, preparing meals for the family becomes a problem—and a cooking class is most welcome. Spanish-speaking women desire to look well and have an eye for style, but they do not have the money with which to buy American clothes. But if someone will teach them to sew, their fingers are nimble, their taste good, and the results are often remarkable. To get what one wants in this country one must speak English, which is a baffling tongue to those who were not born to it. Learning a strange language is an embarrassing business. The greatest possible help is a teacher who is friendly, understanding, and truly a Christian. Many of our customs need interpretation. Why should one consult the doctor about an expected baby, or go to a hospital? If the priest refuses to marry or to bury, what do you do?

And then there are the children. In many Spanish-speaking families it is necessary for the mother as well as the father to work if there is to be enough for everybody to eat. But what are the children to do after school? And if something goes wrong, to whom can they turn? Here the Protestant community center is often the answer. As the children grow older they enter into a world about which their parents know little or nothing. Father and Mother may mean well, but Benito and Margarita are loath to listen to them. Much suffering on both sides can be avoided if there is a friend who understands American life and who can diminish the fears of the older generation and at the same time give some guidance to the younger. The needs of the people carry them past the distrust in which they have been reared to accept the services that Protestantism has to offer.

Protestantism, when it is true to its genius, is an applied religion. It takes much thought for people, all sorts of people. Protestant home missions is far more concerned with helpfulness than with indoctrination. It seeks to lead people to Christ by revealing the spirit of Christ in daily life. On that basis it is both needed and welcome everywhere.

Alberto Rembao, international Christian educator and writer.
Since 1931 he has been editor of *La Nueva Democracia.*

) CHAPTER 2 (

The Spaniards Came First

THE FIRST Europeans to make their way into widespread areas of our country came from Spain. Between 1539 and 1542 DeSoto ranged northward from Florida into the Carolinas, and then westward to the Mississippi. There he died, but his followers made their way down the river and back to Mexico. In 1606 the flag of Spain was carried northward from Mexico to the site of the present city of Santa Fe on the high plateau of the Rockies. This was a year before the English made their first permanent settlement at highly accessible Jamestown on the Virginia coast. Albuquerque had its beginnings in 1706, San Antonio in 1718. While the thirteen colonies were proclaiming their independence, the Spanish were establishing themselves in San Francisco Bay. In 1781 Los Angeles was a little town with a big name (El Pueblo de Nuestra Señora La Reina de los Angeles de Porciuncula) while the site of what is now Chicago was nothing but a swamp.

Courage, perhaps inspired by the love of gold, was the first characteristic of these Spanish pioneers. They delighted in going where men had never been before. They had great physical stamina, else they would not have survived. They got themselves across rivers and over mountains in a way that commands our admiration. Even with all modern conveniences it is a bit difficult to get to some of the spots where they set up crosses and unfurled their flags. And how did they manage to find something to eat? And how did they set their course through the wilderness so as to get back to where they had started? They were often cruel and frequently quarrelsome, but their sheer valor compels our admiration.

In much of our country they left little save their footprints as a possible guide to later comers. They gave us Saint Augustine as our oldest settlement, but until the railroad arrived it developed little. In California they built missions that still delight the tourists, they established land titles on a semimonopolistic basis, they supplied the basis for many colorful but highly synthetic local celebrations. Nobody seems to know what has become of the descendants of the first settlers in Florida. In California some of them became wealthy by selling their real estate, but nothing indicates that any of them have multiplied greatly.

The one place where the old stock has thrived is in the mountains of what is now New Mexico. Here is to be found both the oldest and the purest Spanish blood in the United States. Old World customs were superimposed on Indian traditions and the two blended into a distinctive whole. The encircling mountains isolated the colony from the other Spanish dependencies, and Spanish officials lowered a virtual iron curtain to keep out influences from the north. For three centuries these people kept company with the past; only in the last few years has modern life caught up with them.

Dr. J. T. Reid writes:

And a remarkable people they are in many respects, remarkable not only for their tenacious racial qualities and customs, but for their unique history as well. For more than two centuries they were a "lost people," isolated in the hinterlands of New Spain, forgotten by warring Mother Spain in the seventeenth and eighteenth centuries, neglected by Mexico with its newly won independence after 1821, and finally all but ignored for three quarters of a century after we had gobbled them up in 1848.

When the English settlers on the eastern coast of this continent were founding Jamestown and beating their way into the wilderness of the Ohio Valley and stampeding into the open places of the "wild west," these Spanish settlers of the Rio Grande Basin were conquering hostile Indians, working mines, establishing huge ranches of sheep and cattle, raising crops on the right valley lands, setting up schools and churches, and otherwise adapting their European culture to the emergencies of a frontier land that had only so much to offer.

Under the medieval system by which they lived, with *ricos* and *haciendados* ruling, more or less independently, over vast grants of land and hundreds of slaves and servants, these Spanish pioneers developed an economy that fitted the soil and took care of their needs. They were a proud and self-reliant people.

Then in the latter part of the nineteenth century came the squatters and the cattlemen and the outlaws from the states, and competition and exploitation. Progress plodded its inevitable, stubborn way. A militant, forceful, reckless race of men met a proud, lost remnant of landed barons grown soft with easy living. In less than fifty years much of the land and other property had changed hands. The Spanish settlers were ill-equipped to meet the issue, for many reasons—the type of decadent life they had fallen into, lack of a driving response to the challenge of an expanding frontier, limited resources and credit for new enterprises, lack of functional education, and others.

The result has been a gradual increase of poverty with its attendant ills.

There are in the Southwest some two million of these Spanish-speaking citizens of the United States, who are proud of their allegiance to the Stars and Stripes, who fought valiantly for this country in its two recent wars, and who have contributed much of intrinsic value to the culture and growth of this their native land.

But they are a linguistic minority. Most of them speak Spanish as a native tongue, hold ardently to traditional customs inherited from the past, and find it difficult to make a cultural transition to the American way of life. The education provided in the public schools, though consistent with general practice elsewhere in the country, has been inadequate and ill-suited to their needs, resulting in a lowered educational status and the disadvantages that such a condition brings.

They live among their peaks with their handicaps—poverty, sickness, superstitions and ignorance.[1]

This issue the Protestant churches sought to meet with a classic example of pioneer missionary work. In the second half of the nineteenth century word got around that here was a group of people living under our flag who had no schools. Various denominations heard the call and sent schoolteachers to these remote villages that are known as "plazas" (although often they have no plaza, or square) to gather the children together and teach them to read. By so doing they achieved far more than just introducing book learning. These mission schools were the forerunners of the public schools. The Protestant churches nudged first the territorial and later the state governments toward their duty in the field of public education. More than this, these schools broke the unquestioned control of the pattern of life that the Roman Catholic Church had enjoyed for two and a half centuries. Some of the teachers were also preachers. All of them were the exponents of a vigorous evangelical faith. In New Mexico the Protestant church was built beside the mission school. The combination meant a more abundant life for the people. The teacher and/or the preacher brought some knowledge of hygiene and often a more effective way of tilling the soil. Wholesome recreation came to the young people. Life grew cleaner and brighter.

Meanwhile the world was creeping up on the mountains. First came

[1] *It Happened in Taos*, by J. T. Reid. Albuquerque, University of New Mexico Press, 1946. Used by permission.

the railroad, which thundered on past to the Pacific Coast. In its wake followed the automobile with its much higher power of penetration into what the state automobile tags proclaim to be "The Land of Enchantment." The Governor's Palace in Santa Fe became a museum and the town a show place for California-bound motorists. The artists discovered and embellished Taos. Albuquerque grew from a railroad town to a city of considerable distinction, with the University of New Mexico becoming a cultural center with a strong interest in the people and customs of the hinterland.

The new highways and the people who traveled over them affected the secluded villages in several ways. They created a market for their handicrafts, such as the Chimayo blankets. Jobs developed along the roadsides in filling stations and overnight accommodations. The highways were arrows pointing toward the cities, with Albuquerque the immediate destination. Here the large Spanish-speaking population has not come from south of the border to any considerable degree but has moved in from the surrounding valley.

Then came the atomic bomb. It was in New Mexico that the first bomb was detonated, and it is in New Mexico that it has probably had its greatest local effect. All atomic centers are places apart, hard to get into and operated by people from afar. Los Alamos, however, has profoundly affected the countryside for a hundred miles around. To the descendants of the ancient Spanish settlers Los Alamos has offered jobs, and the jobs have paid real money. Workers, not necessarily on the bomb itself but in the settlements growing out of the bomb, have been recruited from far back in the mountains. Housing being scarce in all the new settlements, these people live at home and work where work is to be had, either in Los Alamos or the other booming towns about it. Instead of changing from one mode of life to another they have both retained the old and added the new. They still live in their ancestral homes, tilling their fields and tending their animals as of old. But every working day the more able-bodied and ambitious drive off to do their part in the life of the mid-century. The immediate result is that they come home with far more money than they have ever known before. The long range effect will probably be to weaken their traditional way of living, but as yet that is not too apparent. For the moment the big change is in their financial status.

But the new day has its shadows. The same forces that have brought prosperity to these Spanish-speaking villages have also drawn into the same region those who do not appreciate their traditions and who are inclined to look askance at their dark Spanish features. The transferred workers and the footloose from everywhere have come to the mountains to work on the bomb, and they have brought with them prejudices that flower into discrimination against the people who have lived here for three centuries. For these long-time residents an injured pride has been part of the price that they have paid for pockets overflowing with dollars. Prosperity has threatened their self-esteem. As yet the surface changes have been too new and dazzling for these deeper implications to be too troublesome, but some unhappy days may lie ahead.

Another element in the picture is the ex-GI. The draft took thousands of boys from the mountains, put them into uniforms, and sent them out to the ends of the earth. Many never came back. They found work and greater opportunities elsewhere. Some returned quite unchanged. As one observer put it, "The chief difference is that now they drive to their Penitente meetings in Cadillac cars." A third group are those who have tried to adjust to life in the larger world but who have been unable to do so. They have drifted back to the mountains because there was nowhere else for them to go. They are defeated men and no asset to their communities.

Over against these new elements certain old facts continue. Forty per cent of the people of New Mexico are Spanish-speaking. Ability to use the Castilian tongue is most helpful to office seekers. Spanish is still a legal language in New Mexico. The people who speak Spanish have a larger proportion of the votes than anywhere else in our country. They feel that "We are the people." This very pride creates difficulties. The old families feel no pressing obligation to master English, and yet without a good command of English their children cannot make their way in the present day world.

The changing scene has brought changes in Protestant missionary activity. Where the state and local communities have accepted the responsibility for education, and where the public schools can be carried on without garbed sisters on the faculties and Roman Catholic domination of school boards, mission schools have usually been withdrawn. Those that have been continued, which are a minority of those once operated, are maintained for a number of reasons. In some instances public schools are still not accessible to isolated families. In other instances the public schools may be of poor quality or under Roman Catholic control. On the positive side, the mission schools have trained the ministers and lay leaders of the Protestant churches, and may be expected to continue to do so in future. They are closely related to local churches. Often they bring to the community a needed health service. They pioneer in kindergartens for children and education for adults. They serve their communities in many ways.

Mission schools are maintained in New Mexico by the Presbyterian Church, U.S.A., the Woman's Division of Christian Service of the Methodist Church, and the Evangelical United Brethren Church. They serve what has been described as a double minority: first, a group that has been set apart from the rest of the nation by blood and language; second, the Protestant minority within the Spanish-speaking population. These schools are a means of maintaining the dignity and increasing the competence of both minorities. In addition to the common problems of education they face unusual tasks in the areas of language, diet, and social adjustment.

Some parents of the young people who attend these schools have had little education, and consequently they speak a colloquial or archaic form of their native tongue. "One of our great needs is for someone who can teach our pupils good Spanish," we were told at one school. The lack of grammatical training and a hazy notion of the meanings of words make the mastery of English even more difficult than it would ordinarily be.

Dinner, or the midday lunch, can be quite an educational opportunity. "These young people have been brought up on beans and bread," as one dietitian put it. "Our job is to introduce them to salads and to develop in them an appetite for other vegetables, which is really quite a chore." Health begins with a wholesome diet.

The Presbyterian Church, U.S.A., operates a complete educational system. At one time or another it has had fifty village schools. Of these, six are still functioning. Three are on main highways, two are a bit remote, while the one at Truchas is on a mountain plateau at an elevation of 9,000 feet and is difficult to reach when the dirt road is wet. These schools send their students on to Allison-James, a coeducational junior high boarding school on a spacious campus at Santa Fe. From here they go to Menaul, a senior high boarding school on the outskirts of Albuquerque. Graduates of the school can continue to live there and earn at least a part of their room and board while attending the University of New Mexico. Usually there are about fifteen young people in this group. Thus a clear road is kept open from the first grade in a mountain valley to the university in New Mexico's largest city. Over this Christian highway of learning have traveled many who are now ministers and teachers, business and professional people, leaders in the churches. The aim of this comprehensive system of education is to make a personal faith in Jesus Christ the eventual experience of every pupil.

The Evangelical United Brethren Church has a similar system, which centers in the tiny village of Santa Cruz—a truly rural setting. Here is located the McCurdy School, which has all the grades plus a four year boarding high school. Associated with it are three village schools that send their graduates on to it. Here the evangelical influence is strong. Half of the 204 members of the McCurdy Church are students, and of these 30 have decided to devote their lives to Christian service. Twenty-two who had previously become Life Work Recruits are now attending college. In the local county are 47 public schoolteachers who were trained at McCurdy.

Harwood Girls' School in Albuquerque is conducted by the Woman's Division of Christian Service of the Methodist Church for girls who lack good school facilities at home, or who have no real homes. In addition to the Spanish-speaking girls, there are those of Italian, Syrian, Russian, and Japanese parentage. The modest tuition fees can be paid in farm produce or by the labor of the girl herself. The teachers and students conduct a community center and also run a church vacation school in the Mexican town of Cabezon. A Harwood girl writes, "I have learned that not only preachers, missionaries, and Christian workers can be good Christians, but that we in our simple lives can also follow the Christ-like way. Not everybody has the privilege of hearing Dorothy Maynor, the Negro soprano, in person or of seeing Yehudi Menuhin produce sounds from his violin which lift you up to heaven. Harwood has made it possible for me to see and hear these artists as well as many others."

The Protestant churches have responded to the health needs of New Mexico by establishing two hospitals.

On the highway between Santa Fe and Taos the Presbyterian Church, U.S.A., has a grade A hospital at Embudo at the foot of a steep reddish-brown hillside looking over open fields and·a big highway to another ridge of striking formation thrust up sharply from the sloping fields. It is a twenty-five bed hospital, specializing in the care of women and children, although men patients are also received. It includes, in addition to the one-story hospital building, a nurses' residence, a doctors' house, and several small buildings. Dr. Sarah Bowen, with few intervals of relief, was the only doctor on the staff for a number of years, though a second doctor has now been appointed. Seven nurses, six ward aides, a dietitian, and laboratory and office workers complete the total staff.

This small hospital, with the dispensary and out-clinics, cares for as many as 4,500 patients a year. Sometimes a woman whose first four or five children were born in her plaza home with neighbors to help comes somewhat distrustfully for the sixth to the hospital, and afterwards wonders why she waited so long. Others come for the first and all others. Children are brought in who are undernourished. However, there is definite improvement in general health conditions, as county and state health agencies, the Red Cross, and the public schools, as well as the mission forces, all have their part in raising the level.

Daily evangelistic services, a Bible and a hymnal in Spanish beside each bed, the Christian quality of the staff members, the frequent visits of the pastor from nearby Dixon, the whole atmosphere of service in the name of Christ, make Embudo Hospital one of the strong Christian influences of the region.

Two years ago, it became apparent that the village of Truchas was suffering from a lack of consistent medical care, and the people banded together to put up the adobe building that now houses a regular clinic. Some contributed time to make adobe blocks; men and women alike worked at building the walls of the clinic. Village men made the wooden beams, and the women plastered over the adobe bricks with mud, as is the customary practice. Inside, the clinic is provided with examining tables, sterilizer, supplies of modern drugs. The medical staff from Embudo Hospital (about 25 miles away) goes once a week for consultation. In between, the registered nurse attached to the mission school, capable and conscientious Miss Frances Sanchez, looks after minor and emergency ills and makes needed referrals to the medical staff.

A companion story to Truchas is that of Penasco. Here there has been no Protestant school. Years ago, when medical work was first instituted in the plaza country, a Presbyterian doctor was attacked and almost killed. More recently the Embudo Hospital staff has carried on periodic clinics in makeshift quarters. When word of the clinic at Truchas got around, the people of Penasco, Roman Catholic and Protestant alike, joined in a request for a similar building in which both a clinic and a community program are carried on.

In May, 1948, the Evangelical United Brethren Church dedicated a new hospital where abundant sunlight shines through large, modern windows upon the newest in equipment. It has a staff of thirty-five members from several states and two Canadian provinces whose missionary zeal has brought them to New Mexico. It is located on a hill overlooking the town of Española through which multitudes of workers on the atomic bomb pass daily on their way to Los Alamos. During its first three years this hospital was the scene of almost a thousand births, besides taking care of over five thousand other patients. One of the doctors spends half his time conducting clinics in surrounding towns in cooperation with a full-time visiting nurse. Together they penetrate into the mountains to communities that are not reached by either private physicians or the state health service.

The church is the most widespread Protestant institution in New Mexico. Many congregations are the outgrowth of mission schools that have now given way to public schools. Their first achievement was to break the religious monopoly that had long been enjoyed by the Roman Catholic Church. They have also been effective in prodding that institution toward a better service to its people. But the function of Protestantism is only incidentally competitive.

The following statement is in the Findings of the National Home Missions Congress of 1950: "We recognize our Protestant responsibility for Christian nurture and evangelism among the non-Christian and the nominal Christian groups in our country. A large part of the Spanish-speaking population is unchurched and without Christ. Most of them claim allegiance to the Roman Catholic Church, but very many have actually neglected the faith of their fathers and many more are not even nominal Catholics, much less Christian. They are the so-called 'liberals' but really 'Pagans'."

Although the response to Protestant religious teaching is not startling, particularly numerically, it does have power. This is shown in two churches that we visited.

In Santa Fe we found a church that in a year and a half had grown from five to fifty members and that was in process of erecting a building. The pastor was born in Mexico of Roman Catholic family. He came to this country as a youngster, and was converted by reading the Bible in a hospital. He earned his way while getting an education by taking care of a church, running an elevator, and painting houses. Finally he achieved a master's degree.

The possibilities of the self-supporting Spanish-speaking church are illustrated by the Methodist church of El Buen Samaritano in Albuquerque, which has a good building on a prominent location in the center of the city. Here we found a number of lay people at work in the evening improving its already excellent facilities. The young pastor was born in the Rio Grande Valley of Texas on land that his family had originally secured as a grant from the King of Spain. He was converted at the age of eighteen and attended the Lydia Patterson Institute in El Paso and Trinity University in San Antonio. He confessed that in Texas he had been proud of his Mexican ancestry, but that in Albuquerque he found it wise to say little about it.

His church has been self-supporting since 1943, and with a membership of 500 is raising a budget of $11,000. Three men are giving $5.00 a week to the support of the church, while others are contributing $4.00 and $3.50 weekly. The congregation uses 125 sets of pledge envelopes. Among the members of the church are the assistant to the superintendent of schools, the secretary to Senator Chavez, three public accountants, a school principal, the head of the Spanish department in the schools, some union leaders, several teachers, and twelve university students.

Many churches like this one are attaining maturity in program and self support. They are also producing leadership of quality able to direct and extend their own affairs.

Thus are the descendants of the Spanish settlers of three centuries emerging into the American life of the day. Of these people, it is said that they did not pass over the border, but that the border passed over them. In the coming years they need to become increasingly adjusted to the national life. Protestant missions have opened to them the door of educational opportunity. For today and tomorrow we should help them to adjust spiritually to the world in which they are now living. This is a difficult and demanding task.

Brooke Baldwin

The citizen of Mexican antecedents is eager to make his full
contribution to the life of his community.

) CHAPTER 3 (

Mexico in Texas

IN TEXAS the restless, land-hungry, westward surging tide of American settlers first encountered the more easygoing landholding Mexicans. Here they met, mingled, and then fought at the much remembered Alamo. Some months later the Americans won the Battle of San Jacinto, which established the independence of Texas.

These unfortunate beginnings have somewhat colored the relations of the two groups ever since. Although more people of Mexican extraction live in Texas than in any other state, there has also been more fear and ill will between them and their American neighbors than elsewhere. Fortunately, this situation is beginning to change. Intelligent efforts are being made to improve Mexican-Anglo relations in Texas. Yet our largest state does not change easily. Nowhere are Americans and Mexicans more of a problem to each other.

Geography explains much of what has happened in Texas. The state has no natural Eastern boundary. When the frontier of American settlement got to western Louisiana, there was nothing to stop it from going farther. The land was good, and it could be bought for little money from those who had been given their titles by the King of Spain. Such an illusory and utterly invisible thing as an international boundary line could not restrain the American pioneer stock. During the early decades of the nineteenth century they wandered west and south into this promising land until they outnumbered the Mexicans who had originally possessed it.

A second significant fact is that Texas is a thousand miles from the seat of Mexican rule in Mexico City and that the first two hundred miles south of the Rio Grande is unprepossessing desert. In the 1830's Texas was on the far periphery of Mexican power—and that power was exceedingly weak. The most astonishing fact about the Battle of San Jacinto is that the Mexican General—and President—was able to get something that looked like an army that far from home. Santa Anna deserves credit for that achievement, and it will be cheerfully granted by anyone who has been through the country over which he had to make his way.

On the other hand, the arid region beyond the Rio Grande has been the political salvation of our southern neighbor. The reason that American occupation stopped at its northern bank is that settlers from the north and east could see no conceivable reason for crossing over to the southern bank. Her northern deserts have been Mexico's real protection against American settlers.

The nature of the Rio Grande has also had its effect upon Texas. This river is one of the most significant boundaries in the world. It makes a lot of difference which bank one lives on. Here two civilizations meet. To the south the Indian dominates; to the north the Anglos[1] hold power. To the south the laws, religion, and culture came from

[1] Popular term for "Anglo-Americans."

Spain; to the north they are European. To the south poverty and ignorance have prevailed through most of the years for most of the people; to the north every man is supposed to get ahead and every child to have an education. In few parts of the world does an international boundary line mean so much.

Between these two utterly dissimilar countries lies the Rio Grande, one of the world's strangest rivers. Its name means "big river," but its distinction lies in its length rather than in its depth. From source to mouth it is 1,800 miles, of which half lies between Texas and Mexico, but it is a rare drop of water that ever gets from the mountains of Colorado to the Gulf of Mexico. It flows through arid regions where the sun takes away more moisture than the clouds bestow. In recent years what little water there was has been eagerly diverted into irrigation ditches. During much of the year most of the river is a dry bed, with possibly a brook-like stream meandering down the middle. The Rio Grande peters out rather completely long before it gets to Brownsville.

The international boundary line between the United States and Mexico can properly be described as porous. It operates like a one-way sieve. For reasons already stated, it has served to keep the North Americans out of Mexico, but it has been far less successful in keeping the Mexicans out of the United States. With so many disadvantages to the southward and so many seemingly glistening opportunities to the northward it was inevitable that the more venturesome Mexicans would cross over into what looks and sounds like a modern Promised Land, even if it does not flow with milk and honey. From 1910 to 1920 this movement was accentuated by the disorders of that revolutionary decade in Mexico. As we will see later, there have been many times when influential forces north of the border were eager to have Mexicans cross over, legally or illegally, to help them.

Although the Mexican population immediately south of the border is relatively scant, the Mexicans are a mobile people. While migrants may come a long way to get to the boundary line, it takes only a step to get them across. This has had two curious results. In Texas, the area to a hundred miles north of the Rio Grande is usually far more Mexican than American in population. Those who drive down the Pan-American highway really meet Mexico as soon as they leave San Antonio, judging by road signs, language, and people. The second strange fact is that the Mexican population is much heavier on the north bank of the Rio Grande than on the south bank. As a barrier between nations, the river is a dismal failure!

Behind the present situation along the Rio Grande lies a long story. Putting it in a sentence, the Mexicans first retired before the incoming tide of American settlers and then slowly returned in what have now become overwhelming numbers. For these movements of population there have been several reasons.

In the negotiations of the Treaty of Guadalupe Hidalgo that finally brought peace between the two countries, the Mexican Government was more concerned about the rights of their people who were passing under the sovereignty of the United States than it was with the details of the boundary. Those who did not claim Mexican citizenship within a limited time became citizens of the United States automatically, and theoretically at least enjoyed all the rights of such. The Spanish land titles were confirmed.

A few Mexicans shared actively in the government of the Republic of Texas, and one of the first senators that the state of Texas sent to Washington was of Spanish-speaking ancestry. Some families of wealth and position entered heartily into the new regime. More, however, sold their lands to Americans for what now appear to be pitiful sums, although these were much higher than the prices they had paid for them. In general, the Mexican population of Texas receded into the background for at least fifty years after its incorporation into the United States. And when they "came back," it was not as landowners, but as the humblest of workers.

The original occupation of the Mexicans in Texas was the care of livestock. The American cowboy is indebted to them for his skills, his equipment, and most of his lingo. "Cowboy" is a literal translation of the Spanish term *vaquero* and was first used in Texas in 1836. The terms ranch, bronco, lasso, burro, quirt, stampede, vamoose, mesa, canyon, rodeo, corral, sombrero, loco, all come from the Spanish language by way of Texas. Along with them came much know-how in the handling of cows, the breeding and breaking of horses, and the tending of sheep. Men of Mexican descent still follow these lines of work in Texas and in the Southwest generally. The Spanish term for sheepherder is "pastor." As a worker with livestock the Mexican has a splendid reputation for pastoral reliability and faithfulness. Animals worth many thousands of dollars are entrusted to his care for long periods of time with complete confidence. Many years ago a South Texas farmer told the writer, "A Mexican will work better if you don't watch him than if you do!" At the higher levels of skill, the system of branding cattle is Mexican in its origins, while Mexicans still shine in the demanding but relatively well paid trade of sheepshearing.

The change from cattle raising to farming has greatly increased the demand for Mexican labor in Texas but has drastically lowered its status.

Over the years the reign of King Cotton has been dependent in an increasing degree for its success upon the backbreaking exertions of the lowly Mexican with his wife and children toiling beside him. At the close of the War between the States, Texas' 182,000 slaves constituted one-third of the population. For the most part they became sharecroppers raising cotton. Not until 1890 did the Mexicans begin to enter the cotton fields. They did not come as sharecroppers or as tenants, but as cotton pickers following the season from place to place. Two circumstances sounded the knell of cotton tenancy: the rise in the price of land, which began about 1920; and the advent of the tractor. The family-sized cotton patch became uneconomic under these conditions. Thousands of both Negroes and whites were "tractored off" the soil in the manner so unforgettably described in the opening pages of *The Grapes of Wrath*. Between 1930 and 1940 the number of share-croppers in Texas declined from 205,122 to 39,821, while the average acreage in a cotton farm went up from 251.7 to 329.4 in the same period.[2] Cotton also moved west and northward toward the Panhandle, with great cattle ranges being turned into cotton fields. The cultivation was done with tractors and the picking by migrant workers imported for a short period in the fall.

The mechanization and expansion of cotton cultivation in Texas would have been impossible without large quantities of cheap Mexican labor. As far back as 1926 a Texan told the House Committee on Immigration and Naturalization:

Mr. Chairman, here is the whole situation in a nutshell. Farming is not a profitable industry in this country, and in order to make money out of it, you have to have cheap labor. In order to allow landowners to make a profit off their farms, they want to get the cheapest labor that they can find, and if they get the Mexican labor, it enables them to make a profit. That is the way it is along the border, and I imagine that is the way it is anywhere else.

For the most part, cotton has offered the Mexican seasonal and migratory employment. The usual pattern begins with cotton picking in the lower Rio Grande Valley in early summer, north to Corpus

[2] *Latin Americans in Texas,* by Pauline R. Kibbe, p. 170. Albuquerque, University of New Mexico Press, 1948.

Christi in July and August, then north to the central part of the state and then westward on to the great plains for October, November, and December, and then back to the Rio Grande Valley. According to the Texas Employment Service, 1937 was the peak year for participation in this great trek on the part of Latin Americans, with somewhere between 250,000 and 400,000 men, women, and little children making at least part of this circuit.

The mechanization of cotton has carried over from the method of cultivation to its human relations.

Generally speaking, the Latin American migratory worker going into west Texas is regarded as a necessary evil, nothing more nor less than an unavoidable adjunct to the harvest season. Judging by the treatment that has been accorded him in that section of the state, one might assume that he is not a human being at all, but a species of farm implement that comes mysteriously and spontaneously into being coincident with the maturing of the cotton, that requires no upkeep or special consideration during the period of its usefulness, needs no protection from the elements, and when the crop has been harvested, vanishes into the limbo of forgotten things— until the next harvest season rolls around. He has no past, no future, only a brief and anonymous present.[3]

A third development that has drawn hundreds of thousands of Mexicans across the Rio Grande has been the transformation of the lower Rio Grande Valley from an arid desert raising nothing but brush to a winter garden supplying the nation with citrus fruits and a great variety of vegetables.

This has been made possible by irrigation. The word itself is of Latin origin and we are indebted to our southern neighbors for the laws by which it is administered, for the techniques by which it works, and for the labor that has made it possible.

Large scale irrigation became possible in 1902 when Congress passed the Reclamation Act. The railroad got to Brownsville in 1904. At this

[3] *Ibid.*, page 176. Used by permission.

time the standard of living of our nation was rising rapidly. More varied and more nutritious foods were in demand, while the refrigerator car and the tin can were bringing increasing quantities of fruits and vegetables to the dining rooms of America. At the same time the native-born Americans were no longer willing to do hard physical work. Labor saving machinery was still in its infancy. Even today it is less adapted to the production of fruits and vegetables than any other large scale activity. It has been the muscle and sweat of Mexicans that has dug many of the ditches, cleared away the omnipresent brush, and made the soil ready for cultivation.

It was not alone the strength of his arm, but the Mexican's readiness to live on little, that brought about one of the most astonishing agricultural developments of recent years. Irrigation is by nature expensive. The irrigated land of the Rio Grande Valley was greatly overcapitalized. The long haul by fast freight to the cities of the North cost money. The one cheap item was Mexican labor. Without it these other developments would have been long delayed. Astonishing are the wonders that have been wrought.

A Northern visitor driving into the Lower Rio Grande Valley would experience the illusion

> . . . of moving into a modern version of the Garden of Eden. As he drove along the Valley's Main Street, a 65-mile highway, he would see stately palms and green citrus-fruit trees laden with golden orange fruit; bougainvillea vines in full bloom; bright green papaya plants. . . . And when he came to the level, rich fields he would see bronze-skinned people by the thousands harvesting vegetables—red beets with their green tops, white and purple turnips with their green tops, golden carrots with their green tops—everything green. He might see other laborers harvesting cabbage, broccoli, endive, peppers, beans, tomatoes, new potatoes, peas, anise, cauliflower, or squash.[4]

[4] Hart Stilwell, quoted in *North from Mexico,* by Carey McWilliams, pp. 175-76. Philadelphia, J. B. Lippincott Co., 1949. Used by permission.

The value of these crops runs to $100,000,000 a year—of which the men who do the work receive a rather pitiable proportion.

When Texas achieved her independence, 5,000 Mexicans formed one sixth of her population. By 1900 the Mexican population had increased to 70,000. Thirty years later it had jumped to 683,000, and at present it is well over a million—still a sixth of the people of the state.

However, the Spanish-speaking population is unevenly distributed over Texas. Some are found in fabulous Houston and booming Dallas. In El Paso and San Antonio they constitute more than half of the population. Most of the Mexicans in the Lone Star State live south of a line drawn through El Paso and San Antonio and then extended eastward to the gulf at a point somewhat south and west of Galveston. This is the part of Texas that is least attractive to fortune seekers from other parts of the world. Few industries are found here and only two cities of over 100,000 population.

The distribution of Mexicans in Texas is significant in another way. They are more rural than urban; more live in the open country and the small towns than in the cities—a fact that has hindered their progress in several ways, as will be pointed out shortly.

In America the business success and social approval of any group is largely dependent upon fluent use of the English language and adequate education. This cultural hurdle all non-Anglos must negotiate. This has been most difficult for the Spanish-speaking people of Texas, because they have never had a good opportunity to learn the language. This is due to their concentration in certain areas, usually in the small towns and the country, and their employment in tasks in which they work as a group with the minimum of contact with their English-speaking over-bosses. Each gang is recruited by a *capitán* or *jefe* who speaks English. He gets his orders and then tells his workers, in Spanish, what to do.

The pathway from the Mexican home to the American public school is long and hazardous. The home may be a jalopy rattling around from cotton field to cotton field, or even going on some of the longer excursions that will be described later. Any school board finds it difficult to provide facilities for children who are really birds of passage. It is the exceptional schoolteacher who has a cordial welcome for a pupil who is here today and somewhere else tomorrow.

Even though the home be firmly anchored in one spot, there are difficulties. Often the struggle to keep alive is so intense that even the hands of the seven-year-old are needed if the family is to have its daily minimum of *frijoles*. Even beans come hard to the poor. Suitable clothes may be lacking. The way to school may be so long and the child so poorly nourished that he can learn but little when he gets there. The pathway itself is strange. His parents have never traveled it in many cases. Uneducated parents, who have had few agreeable contacts with educated people, do not see value in schooling for their children. They doubt if book learning will materially improve their lot in life. Some may not send them at all, or they may send them only when it is convenient and there is nothing else for them to do.

Other troubles beset the Spanish-speaking child when he passes through the door of the schoolhouse. To him this is a very strange place. To the American child the first grade teacher is a mother substitute to whom he can turn with some assurance of being understood. With the Spanish-speaking child this usually does not work. The teacher may not understand his language. She is alien to him, and he does not trust her. Oftentimes a most unfortunate attitude toward the school is developed by the Spanish-speaking child on his first encounter with it. He does not feel at home. This is not his natural world, and therefore he resists that which it offers. Too often this becomes the habit of his later days.

Then there are other difficulties. The teacher may be lukewarm in her welcome, the other children scornful if not antagonistic. The Spanish-speaking child's clothes or even his lunch may be the object of derision. These things hurt when you are small, and the child of the lowly Mexican has no defenses.

The work of the school may be both difficult and uninteresting. The language must be learned, as well as the usual lessons. Almost inevitably little Benito and his sister Carmencita are retarded. They may be kept in first grade for two or three years, becoming increasingly bored with their lessons and sensitive to their growing height and age in comparison with the other pupils.

Here the picture is complicated by some features peculiar to Texas. Education was not made compulsory in the state until 1916, and the responsibility for its enforcement is wholly local. Because of the lands that she has retained, Texas has the largest state fund for the aid of schools to be found in the Union. For many years this was distributed on the basis of the children enumerated in each school district rather than on the basis of school enrollment or attendance. From the point of view of the school, every child who could be discovered meant dollars from the state, regardless of whether the child had ever even seen the schoolhouse. The way this worked in the smaller communities was that the fewer the Spanish-speaking children who got to school, the more money there was to spend on the English-speaking children. This meant either a better school or a lightened load for the taxpayer. Here was a temptation that many communities could not resist. To state the matter mildly, they did not overexert themselves in their efforts to persuade Mexican children to go to school. Fortunately this has now been corrected by the passage of the Gilmer-Aiken Bill, which requires that state funds be distributed on the basis of actual attendance, but the effects of the former arrangement are still felt.

There has also been a tendency on the part of some local administrations to apply the pattern of segregation to the Mexicans, both in the schools and elsewhere. The linguistic difficulties of the Mexican child and also his alleged lack of cleanliness have been used to justify segregation. Sometimes there have been separate buildings and sometimes separate rooms in the same building. The root motive has been "social customs," which is another name for prejudice. The result has been to set the Spanish-speaking child apart from the other children and to give him a sense of inferiority. Fortunately, there is no legal basis for this segregation, and the United States District Court for the Western District of Texas has ruled that it violates the Fourteenth Amendment to the Constitution.

Honesty demands that full credit and recognition be given to those Texas teachers, principals, and superintendents who through the years have pioneered in giving adequate and equal educational advantages to children of Mexican descent. Their number is large, even though they do constitute a small minority among the thousands of public schoolteachers in Texas. Bucking administrative apathy—even antagonism at times—and confronting more frequently the opposition presented by some Anglo parents who are prompted only by unreasoning and unfounded prejudice, these educators have stuck to their guns, winning out in the end.[5]

Fortunately this tendency to segregation does not go all the way up. Often it stops at the third grade; never does it persist into high school, although there the child of Mexican antecedents may encounter some forms of social ostracism. The colleges of Texas are wide open to sons and daughters of her Spanish-speaking citizens.

The Spanish-speaking child in Texas can have an education if he wants it enough to make somewhat more of an effort than is required of the Anglo child. In the cities, the young people from the more prosperous Mexican homes are nearly on a par with the other boys and girls of the community. While most Spanish-speaking children are

[5] Kibbe, *op. cit.*, p. 103. Used by permission.

under a handicap, which varies with where they live and with their economic position, some of them are climbing all the way to the top.

The state is taking measures to improve conditions.[6] In 1943 the State Department of Education issued a two-point statement of policy, the first of which proposed that the courses of study used in Texas schools be revised so as to give all the children a better appreciation of Latin American history and culture. The second point stated flatly, "Any administrative or curricular practices which isolate, or tend to isolate, the Latin American children solely on the basis of such descent, through physical separation or inequitable educational offerings, are deemed pedagogically unsound, contrary to state and national policy, and inimical to the best interests of both those groups of children." With the financial assistance of the Office of the Coordinator of Inter-American Affairs in Washington a number of conferences and workshops were held under the auspices of the colleges of the state to study the situation and to seek ways of improving it, particularly by training elementary teachers in the use of Spanish and in promoting better community relations. The Governor appointed a Good Neighbor Commission, with offices in the state capitol, which had among its objectives:

To educate our present adult Anglo-American population in the history and culture of Mexico, on inter-American relations, and on the problems faced by Latin Americans in Mexico.

To study the economic and educational opportunities of the Latin American residents of the community, as well as their housing and health conditions, with a view to effecting improvements.

To promote friendship, understanding, and respect between Anglo-Americans and Latin Americans of the community, thereby insuring the continuance of cordial relations between Texas and Mexico.

To investigate fully, in case problems in human relations arise between Anglo-Americans and Latin Americans in the community, and adjust such

[6] *Ibid.*, p. 104.

difficulties with justice to both sides, to the end that strife may be avoided
and understanding promoted.

None of these aims has as yet been fully achieved, but officially
the power of the state and the influence of its educational institutions
is on the side of affording better educational opportunities and social
treatment to its Spanish-speaking population.

Now let us look briefly at the economic and social position of the
Americans of Spanish-speaking ancestry in Texas.

On the lowest level are the agricultural workers, who may be here
legally or illegally and who may be settled or migrant. A large proportion of the recent arrivals from Mexico are in this classification.
Here are the families that have a minimum acquaintance with the
English language, and whose children have few contacts with our
schools.

The Spanish-speaking people of the towns are better off than the
agricultural workers. Most of them can speak some English. Their
range of employment expands to include all sorts of humble but necessary tasks. The children go to school. The boys get jobs and the girls
may clerk in stores.

In the cities, Spanish-speaking Latin Americans are spread over a
wide gamut both economically and socially. In El Paso and San Antonio
are considerable slums occupied by Spanish-speaking people; in Dallas
there is a remnant of such a deteriorated neighborhood. However, the
slum is not the usual dwelling place of the urban Latin Americans of
Texas. As fast as they can, they get themselves bungalows in better and
better neighborhoods. Owing to informal agreements among real estate
interests, it would not be fair to say that they enjoy entirely free choice
as to where they will live, but they have some chance to pick and
choose, particularly in the lower price levels.

The cities offer a wide range of employment in the service trades, industry, business, and the professions, with the women at some levels doing better than the men. The women have quick fingers and excel in the needle trades, and may become department heads in the garment factories that are developing in Dallas.

In the cities many of the young people graduate from high school, many of the boys becoming bank clerks and the girls stenographers. Public health nursing is open to those who can go further, and the professions generally. Many are active in government and politics, some having been elected to high state and national offices.

On the business side, the natural starting point is the small neighborhood grocery store, known as a *bodega*, specializing in Spanish foods—and language. A further step up is the barbershop, which may serve the Anglo trade. The Mexican eating place is taking on distinction, first as an atmospheric spot appealing to adventurous Anglos, and then simply as a good restaurant where anybody is glad to go. One of the most popular eating places in the best residential section of Dallas is owned and operated by a Mexican. Dallas also boasts six tortilla factories under Mexican ownership and management.

In Texas the social acceptance of a Mexican depends largely on his clothes, the way he carries himself, his use of English, and the amount of money that he has in his pocket. Agricultural workers are discriminated against early and often. The smaller the community the higher the social barriers. "Most instances of refusal of service occur in towns and villages of less than 5,000 population, and those most frequently refused service are in the lower income brackets."[7] A man who has spent his life working with Mexicans put it this way, "If a Mexican is well dressed and enters one of the better eating places with a confident manner and is not heard to speak Spanish, he will be served practically anywhere in Texas." My friend stressed the importance of avoiding the

[7] *Ibid.*, page 217. Used by permission.

use of Spanish in public places in the smaller communities; the sound of a strange language seems to frighten the rural Anglo-Americans! Although they suffer from certain disabilities as a group, it is not difficult for an individual to extricate himself from the discriminations practiced against his fellows. In every social situation there is some sort of an escape hatch.

Most Spanish-speaking Americans of Texas are nominally Roman Catholic. When possible, they desire to be baptized, married, and buried by their traditional church. How much further this affiliation goes depends upon circumstances. The agricultural workers have scant if any contact with the Roman Catholic Church. On the other hand, in cities such as El Paso and San Antonio, Roman Catholic institutions, including the parochial school, enjoy considerable Mexican patronage.

In Texas the investment of Protestant missionary dollars among the Spanish-speaking people has not been at all in proportion to their need. For this there are several reasons. This is not one of the long established mission fields of the church. Most of the Spanish-speaking population of Texas has entered this country during the past twenty-five years. This is a period when our churches have been concerned with the problems growing out of the depression and the greatest of all wars. Upheavals nearer home have kept our attention from such a remote spot as the Rio Grande Valley.

The influx from Mexico has had more of the aspects of a flood than of an ordered migration. Workers came and went and came again as far as the international boundary was concerned. In the local communities north of the border they were distinctly transient. Their low economic status and their roving habits made it difficult to do anything with them or for them—and so little has been attempted.

A successful contact between Protestantism and Mexican newcomers in Texas has been through the Migrant Service of the Division of Home

Missions of the National Council of Churches, which has sent a succession of young people into the lower Rio Grande Valley to do what could be done with the Mexicans who were gathering the vegetables with which to enrich the winter diet of our country. I have seen a graduate of Yale Divinity School teaching English to a group of adult Mexicans by lantern light in the crudest of settlements—and have returned after two hours to find him still holding the attention of his class. I have seen a nurse representing cooperative Protestantism examining the babies of unbelievably young Mexican mothers. I learned that the churches of one of the valley communities had agreed to give $1,000 toward making life tolerable for the Mexicans in their fields.

Like the workers, this work has been highly mobile, with trailers used for living quarters by some of the staff. There has been neither the time nor a favorable situation for thoroughgoing religious instruction. The migrants have been given help that they needed, and in the name and spirit of Christ. Equally important, the local communities have been awakened to some sense of responsibility for these people who toil in their fields when needed and then disappear. In the eyes of some of the local church people, they have moved up from the status of "hands" to that of human beings.

Somewhat similar, but with a bit more local rootage, is the work camp that the Methodists launched at Pharr in the summer of 1950. Here eighteen young people of the Anglo, Mexican, and Negro groups, all with some college training, lived and worked together for six weeks, with "work" running the gamut from ditch-digging to teaching in vacation schools and even preaching. Their devotion shone in such contrasting ventures as painting churches and conducting evenings of hilarious recreation. The result was improved work by the local leaders in the churches and church schools of the Rio Grande Valley in helping newcomers from across the border to make a hopeful adjustment.

The Protestant churches can never ignore the conditions under which people live. The Spanish-speaking people of Texas have been an invitation to humanitarian endeavor. The Mexican Christian Institute that is maintained by the United Christian Missionary Society of the Disciples of Christ in San Antonio illustrates the purposes of a number of similar institutions maintained by various denominations. Mr. E. G. Luna, the head of the institute, was born in Mexico in 1906 and originally came to this country to study for the Mexican consular service, taking degrees at Texas Christian University and the University of Texas. He became head of the institute in 1944.

This is a missionary institution that is addressing its Christian idealism toward the practical goal of improving the conditions among the Mexican people and helping them to find their proper place in the community. It serves 4,000 people a year. Its program starts with health. It has a maternity clinic and campaigns against diarrhea and tuberculosis. It stresses the need for a better diet, plugging for cod liver oil and pablum, and helps the women with their canning, particularly tomatoes and apricots. It asks, "Why be a migrant?" inviting everybody to take a bath, urging the men to wear coats and ties, and helping the women to make better clothes for less money for themselves and their children. The result is increased personal pride, better job opportunities, a higher type of home.

The institute is troubled because only 15,000 out of 150,000 Mexicans in San Antonio care enough about the duties of citizenship to pay the $1.75 poll tax and vote, and because 30,000 Mexicans in the city have failed to secure their naturalization papers. It takes pride in the recent bond issue of $9,000,000 to be used to improve the schools in the Mexican areas.

Mr. Luna states, "The Mexicans can and should solve their own problems. Signs of hope are the 1,700 Mexican young people who finish high school each year in Texas, the many hundreds who are attending college in Texas, and those who are doing graduate work." Although the gospel that he preaches majors on adults learning to read and write, parents sending their children to school regularly, and everybody saving money, this is rated as quite "Protestant" by the Roman Catholic authorities—but "that does not keep the people from coming to us," reports Mr. Luna.

A vacation school conducted by two students from the University of San Antonio in 1937 has led to the establishment of a community center at Ozona, Texas, in the heart of the sheep and goat ranches. It is sponsored by a board representing three denominations and serves a Spanish-speaking population of 1,200 under the direction of two Methodist deaconesses. The Methodist minister reports, "The initiative of these people shows their growth in character. The men built the sidewalk, driveway, and garage at the center, while the women bought the piano, silver, dishes, cooking utensils, linoleum for the kitchen, and curtains for the stage." Through the center better relations have been established with the community, and this has brought more jobs for the young people and an increasing mutual respect.

In Texas conditions have led Protestant home missions to reverse their usual pattern. For the ambitious young person of Spanish-speaking ancestry the doors of the colleges and universities are wide open, which obviates the need for missionary colleges. At the high school level instruction is readily available. The real problem is at the bottom of the educational ladder. The time when the Spanish-speaking child most needs help is when he first starts to school. That is the crucial moment.

Mrs. Alfredo Nanez, wife of the director of religious education for the Rio Grande Conference of Mexican Methodist churches, puts it this way, "Did you ever take two or three courses or even a major in

Spanish and then find yourself in a group of Spanish-speaking people where you could neither speak nor understand the language? Then you may have some idea of how a six-year-old from a Spanish home feels when he first goes to the public school."

The Woman's Division of Christian Service has maintained three kindergartens along the Rio Grande border since 1947. Mrs. Nanez describes their work: "These kindergartens give the child a year or two of language development, which enables him to feel at home in school and thus avoid the problem of retardation. He learns to get along with other children in a free but supervised program. Through play he learns right attitudes toward children of other races and toward his environment."

Interestingly, the church schools that have been established have been aimed at the south bank of the Rio Grande almost as much as at the north bank.

What is popularly known as Pres-Mex (the Presbyterian School for Mexican Girls) is an institution maintained by the Presbyterian Church in the U. S. at Taft, Texas, near Corpus Christi. Its purpose is to train Mexican young women for Christian service. The girls live on their own campus but attend the local high school along with the Anglo boys and girls of the community. The state takes care of their academic training, while the church agency teaches housekeeping and cooperative living. Pres-Mex takes pride in the ministers' and teachers' wives that it has produced.

The big brother to Pres-Mex is Tex-Mex, or more formally the Texas Mexican Industrial Institute at Kingsville, to the south of Corpus Christi. This is also supported by the Presbyterian Church in the U. S. It has 700 acres of what was originally mesquite brush that has been turned into a productive farm and adorned with numerous attractive buildings by the labor of generations of Mexican boys who have been working their way through school and thereby making their way up in the world. Practical training is given in printing, woodworking, welding, plumbing, and other trades, but Christian character is its major aim.

The Lydia Patterson Institute is in the heart of the Mexican section of El Paso and almost in sight of the Mexican boundary. Its students, to the number of 500, come from both sides of the international line. It is supported by the Methodist Church. In addition to offering a good high school education it has a Department of Ministerial Training, with a dozen or so candidates for the ministry distributed through the grades, the high school, and the first year of college. These men are given practical experience along with their school training. Those who are high school graduates attend the Western College of the University of Texas, which is located in El Paso, but live at the institute. From here ministerial students are sent to the Southern Methodist University at Dallas, where there are sixty Latin Americans among the undergraduates and four in the Perkins School of Theology. The Reverend Ben O. Hill, who has spent his life working with Latin Americans of Texas, looks after these Spanish-speaking students.

Another border school is Holding Institute at Laredo, Texas, which attracts boys and girls from as far south as Mexico City and as far north as Chicago. They come from both isolated areas and broken homes. About half of the students are from Roman Catholic homes. A graduate testifies, "I owe Holding for all my schooling through the grades and four years of high school. There I accepted Christ as my personal Saviour under the preaching of Dr. Onderdonk. In my efforts to live the Christian life I have been helped by both the precepts and the example of the teachers at Holding." As high as 50 per cent of the graduates go on to college.

At San Juan, in the heart of the lower Rio Grande Valley, the American Lutheran Church maintains a Bible school for the training of workers with the Mexicans.

The local Protestant church is the place where most Mexicans are most likely to find that which they need. Here it is that they can learn to know and trust a God who cares for them. Here it is that their self-respect is first awakened and then nourished. Here they learn to work with other people. In the church are the springs of eternal life. Through the church the individual can achieve an increasing measure of favor with both God and man.

The local church is the most permanent of missionary institutions. In education the state in the end offers the church impossible competition. In social welfare the local community ultimately assumes its responsibilities. But nothing supersedes the church.

But the local church is also the most difficult of institutions both to found and foster. The reason is simple. Schools and other institutions can be financed and managed from outside, but a church can only succeed in proportion as the people to whom it ministers assume responsibility for it. The church is perhaps the most intimate of human institutions. People must give themselves to it before it can do much for them. For this very reason the Spanish-speaking church has had a hard time and has often made a disappointing record.

The people of Mexico have never been trained in the sort of teamwork that is essential to a successful church. In their local communities they have had few responsibilities. The Roman Catholic Church has decided all religious matters for them. The Spanish tradition is one of individualism rather than cooperation. Where its culture prevails there are few voluntary organizations, and it is an axiom that "committees rarely commit." The spirit of the New England town meeting is utterly alien.

Most of the Spanish-speaking people of the United States are poor.

They have little money with which to support a church and no training whatever in giving.

As we have stressed repeatedly, most of them have few permanent roots in the soil of the United States. A Protestant church presupposes a settled, continuing constituency, and not one that moves around with the crops.

These conditions have made it difficult to recruit and train effective pastors. Here the church faces an almost impossible alternative. If a minister lacks education and is compelled to live on a pittance, he can rarely lead his people far. On the other hand, if he has received college and seminary training and is guaranteed a living wage by his mission board, he is in danger of becoming separated from the people whom he is supposed to serve, and may not be able to lead them at all! A man's effectiveness does not depend upon what he knows, but upon the intimacy of the ties that unite him to his people. For this reason the man with less training may sometimes outshine the man with more training. Against this is raised the question, "Unless a minister knows something, how can he teach his people anything?"

Three policies are followed by the various denominations. The first is to insist upon full college and seminary training for all pastors. The second is to profess this ideal in theory, but not to hold to it too strictly in practice. The third is to take ministers where you can find them and then do what may be possible for them. The last policy seems to achieve the most immediate practical results.

This ministerial supply problem is matched by another similar one in the life of the churches. The people who most need the stimulation that the Protestant church usually brings are the poor, the uneducated, the underprivileged, but as soon as they become a part of the church they proceed to dress up, work their way up in the world, send their children to high school and college, and move away into a better neighborhood. Should a church stay on the job for which it was originally intended, or should it follow its constituency? And unless a church keeps up with the prosperous segment of its constituency, these people, or at least their children, will move over into an Anglo church.

Facing the same problem from another angle, should the educated, privileged person of Latin ancestry continue in a Spanish-speaking church, with its more or less inevitable limitations, or should he slip over into an English-speaking congregation? The argument for staying is that his money and his leadership are needed by his old friends. The argument for moving over is that by so doing he breaks down prejudices that many Anglos carry and commends his people as a group to his new friends. He gives his children a more favorable social setting, and may keep them from deserting the church by so doing. In theory, at least, the sooner we develop unsegregated churches in which several racial groups worship together, the better. The church rarely promotes segregation willingly, but it often finds itself working among segregated people. The appeal of assimilation is great, but it has a dismal sound to the ear of the Spanish-speaking minister who needs both liberal contributors to his budget and people with the education and self-confidence to exercise effective leadership.

Interesting signs of the times in San Antonio are the decision of the son of a Texas-Mexican minister to prepare himself to serve Anglo churches, and the building of an attractive church in a good neighborhood with a retired banker as the pastor, for the avowed purpose of saving to the church the carriage trade that has developed among the Spanish-speaking people of this city. The more a foreign-language church does for its people, the more of them is it likely to lose to English-speaking congregations. In one sense it should live to die, but that takes an abundance of Christian grace and is never an easy assignment.

The Rio Grande Conference of the Methodist Church is the largest Spanish-speaking ecclesiastical organization in the United States. It has three district superintendents, sixty-five pastoral charges, of which eight are in New Mexico, and just under 10,000 members. The conference raises $60,000 a year for local expenses and has 18 self-supporting congregations. Next to poverty, the greatest problem of these churches is the way their people come and go. On the other hand, they minister to youth to a remarkable degree. The families are large and the young people responsive. From 60 to 80 per cent of the people are under thirty-five years of age. Sunday school attendance is large in proportion to membership. Both are growing. Church and Sunday school attendance have doubled in the past fifteen years.

The Methodists and the Presbyterians are the best organized and the largest groups of Spanish-speaking Protestant churches in Texas— but there are many more sponsored by various denominations and by no denomination.

Protestantism has a firm rootage among the Latin Americans of Texas. Spectacular growth is not to be expected, but healthy development is assured. As Protestant people obtain a firmer economic foothold and their children secure a better education, they are certain to increase in influence, probably out of all proportion to their numbers. The over-all situation calls for leadership that will put responsibility upon the people in the churches and yet at the same time inspire them to exercise it in wise ways. Probably the greatest single need is for ministers who combine an education with the common touch, who can meet the standards that our communities set for Protestant pastors but who at the same time can keep the confidence of humble people who labor with their hands and who have little if any education. Where such ministers are found, they are most fruitful both in human good and in the enlargement of the church.

Naomi Blank

Pedro learns quickly when the home missions teacher gives
him a chance and a good friend lends encouragement.

) CHAPTER 4 (

Mexicans in Wonderland

To THE imagination of Mexicans on either side of the border, California seems to be a Promised Land. Here Mexico's discredited politicians take refuge. The late President Plutarco Elías Calles, Mexico's last strong man in the old tradition, spent five years in retirement in San Diego during a period when he was out of political favor at home. In Denver we were told by a Mexican pastor, "When my people take a trip they don't go to Mexico, but to California. That is where they have connections, and that is where their eyes are pointed!" Los Angeles claims to be second only to Mexico City as a center of Mexican population and life.

Yet California is not easily accessible from the populated centers of Mexico. The border is near at hand, but there is nothing south of it save resorts such as Tijuana—where Americans can indulge in more or less illicit pleasures—and great open spaces. The total population of Lower California would soon be lost on the streets of Los Angeles.

There is no connection by rail or highway with the rest of Mexico. The nearest port of entry through which much immigration flows is Nogales, Arizona, which is 572 miles from Los Angeles. Mexicans cannot drift into California in the casual way that they do into Texas. They do not arrive by accident; it takes real effort for them to get to California.

In southern California the Mexicans have played a minor role in one of the great dramas of modern times. They have been behind the scenes in the creation of a new center of world population. Their lowly labor has added much to the splendor of the nation's fourth and fastest growing city, and to the wondrous region round about.

Carey McWilliams has aptly described southern California as an "island on the land." It is surrounded by the ocean, mountains, and deserts. It is not a natural center for either commerce or culture. Southern California's original asset was sunshine, and it is still a basic attraction. Here is a land where people can live out of doors the year around.

Southern California has shown a remarkable ability to find new economic opportunities for the sunshine lovers who have flocked to her. First came the citrus industry, then tourists and health seekers, then the movie industry. Recent years have brought the manufacture of sports clothes, the fabrication of airplanes, and the work of roaring steel mills.

Each development has attracted a new flood of settlers. As Carey McWilliams points out, each tide of population has come a shorter distance and has brought less money with it. First came New England capitalists to invest considerable sums in the growing of citrus fruits. They were followed by the retired Iowa farmers, who at least had enough to live on without too much work. The stream of Mexicans began to flow in 1911, but first stopped and then reversed during the thirties. During the depression years the Okies and the Arkies chugged into the state in their ancient jalopies. And then came the Mexicans.

Although there have always been Spanish-speaking people in California, the large-scale migration from south of the border is a relatively recent development.

In southern California the Mexican immigrant has found a ready-made role awaiting him. He falls into a pattern that is a century old. In the days of the Gold Rush the Chinese appeared to wash the clothes and cook for those who were striving to get rich in a minimum of time. They stayed on to do the hard work in the pioneer settlements. As they saved their money and prospered, they became unpopular, and the Japanese were brought in to take their place. These, in turn, worked hard, bought land, and were discriminated against on a variety of alleged grounds. This pattern was repeated again and again until the Mexicans took over the hard, back-breaking jobs that nobody wanted. Along with their employment, they inherited the prejudices under which their predecessors had suffered.

There are several circumstances that have conspired to keep the Mexican newcomers from entering into the main stream of California life.

The original land grants made by the kings of Spain and confirmed by the Treaty of Guadalupe Hidalgo have been the basis of land tenure in California ever since. Instead of being homesteaded in quarter sections by humble people, as was the case in much of the West, most of the good soil of California has been held in vast tracts by the fortunate few. The uses to which it was put—first cattle and then fruit—were conducive to large scale operations. The result has been what Carey Mc-Williams has described as "factories in the field"—production line techniques applied to agriculture.

The Mexican stepped into this picture not as an individual but as a "hand," a member of a gang taking orders from a Spanish-speaking boss. The rule in southern California has been to hire a lot of Mexicans or none at all. Chances of promotion are scant and the contacts with American workers almost non-existent.

Along with segregation in work has gone segregation in living quarters. Poor pay has meant poor homes. The traditional pattern has been the *colonia,* a small cluster of substandard huts on the wrong side of something—a railroad, river, *arroyo,* highway, or hill—restricted solely to Mexicans. Such settlements are characteristic of southern California, although usually tucked away in such a fashion as not to attract the notice of the traveler. There is said to be such a community within a mile and a half of Los Angeles' ornate Civic Center. Usually the lines are sharply drawn about such groups. Poorer class Mexicans have few if any American neighbors. Their contacts are with their own people.

This separateness has been further accentuated by the attitudes of the people whose places they have taken in the economic scheme of things. The rapid growth of southern California has brought together a lot of people in a hurry. Many have sought its sunshine because they were not doing too well in the places from which they came. This has been particularly true of the large migration from the Southern states to Los Angeles. These people are rootless and insecure. They have many new neighbors but few old friends. Their church ties are tenuous. They are eager for emotional outlets, and have fallen an easy prey to political charlatans and fake messiahs. They are looking for someone to look down on, and are predisposed to hate. The Mexicans, being on a lower rung of the ladder than they, have been an easy target for their prejudices. These were manifested in the zoot suit riots and other similar occurrences.

Inevitably, this situation has had an unhappy effect upon the Mexicans who have newly come to this country. They find themselves in a strange and dazzling land, but their jobs are usually seasonal and their living quarters unsatisfactory. Insecurity faces them on every side.

They distrust employers, landlords, and anyone in authority, having had little experience with friendly public officials and no knowledge of social agencies such as are found in American cities. The Mexican immigrant withdraws from the larger life about him. His interests center in his own countrymen and pre-eminently in his family.

How to feed himself and his children is the problem that constantly confronts him. Not knowing the language, with his strong arms and nimble fingers as his chief asset, having no knowledge or experience with either industrial or agricultural machinery, he is compelled to take the jobs that nobody else wants. Much of this is "stoop labor." At the end of the day he is too exhausted with his arduous toil to be concerned about much more than something to eat and a place to sleep.

His numerous children are the ultimate salvation of many a Mexican, in that they help him to adjust to American life as does nothing else, but they are an immediate economic burden. The Mexican consul in a Midwestern city put it this way: "If an American gets only three thousand dollars a year, he has just one child. When he gets a raise to four thousand, he has a second, and when his pay goes to five thousand he may have a third. But a Mexican does not do it that way. If he loses his job, he is likely to have two children more to add to those already on hand!" Just getting enough to feed the family is the first concern of most Mexicans during their early years north of the border.

Yet from these lowly beginnings the Mexicans and their children are going far in southern California. The disabilities from which they suffer are temporary rather than permanent, and there appear to be no hurdles that some young American of Mexican ancestry cannot get over.

The very newness of southern California helps. In the long established steel mills of South Chicago the Poles have pre-empted the good jobs, leaving the hottest and dirtiest work for the Mexicans. In the new steel mills of southern California there are no such vested interests, and the Mexicans have a better chance for the work that pays real money. Truck driving is another new field where they are getting a good foothold. As the children go through high school and the more ambitious boys and girls manage to go on to college, they spread out into all manner of occupations and callings. Real estate and law are two areas where they are conspicuously present. The children of Mexican immigrants have traveled far from the place where they started.

This is reflected in where they live. Some Mexicans live in all but the most expensive areas of Los Angeles, but the chief concentration is in East Los Angeles. Part of this area is outside the city limits and therefore lacks some of the usual urban services, such as pavements, street cleaning, libraries, etc. Most of the buildings are forty years old. The prevailing type of house is the one-story bungalow that was particularly beloved by young American couples who were not too well off in the years before the first world war. The people who built these humble homes have prospered and moved elsewhere; the Mexicans have inherited them. The property has not deteriorated as much with the years as one might expect. Many homes are well kept without and immaculate within.

The principle that largely governs where the Mexicans live in southern California is the amount of money in their pockets. They get the best homes that they can pay for. This means rent to begin with, but ownership later in many cases. When they get more money, they will live in better houses. It is as simple as that. Also, these finer abodes will be scattered over the city. The present concentrations of Mexicans are not due to inherent clannishness, but to their common poverty. Since the world began poor people, whatever their nationality, have had to live together. As they escape from the limitations imposed by the lack of coin of the realm, they will mingle more with the larger community.

Mounting prosperity is multiplying the contacts between the Mexicans of southern California and the Roman Catholic Church.

In Los Angeles the Mexicans are achieving an economic level at which church support is possible. When poor people get money, among their first luxuries are elaborate church weddings.

The parochial school has long enrolled Mexican children in Los Angeles and in the other cities with a sizable Mexican population. The pastor of a Mexican Methodist church reported the arguments being used to persuade Mexican parents to send their children to parochial schools: "Public schoolteachers smoke, they drink, they run around at night and sometimes arrive at school the next morning weary and unprepared. The nuns who teach in the parochial schools lead orderly lives. At night they study their lessons for the next day, say their prayers, go to bed early, get up, pray some more, and arrive in the schoolroom with refreshed bodies, clear heads, and well prepared lessons ready to teach your children." For Mexican fathers and mothers who are distrustful of American life and ways, this is a convincing line of reasoning, which may be reinforced with allusions to sin and purgatory.

In the Los Angeles area the variety of Protestant churches ministering to Mexicans is most impressive. Their constituencies run the gamut from the minority who are hungry and homeless to the majority who are on their way up economically. In the western portion of the city there is at least one well built, well maintained church catering to a well-to-do congregation. In East Los Angeles some of the buildings have been inherited from English-speaking congregations. In addition, there are a number of stucco and wood buildings designed for their present occupants.

The range of emphasis is equally wide. A social worker in a church-supported center stated, "Language is the greatest handicap under which these young people suffer; one of our big jobs is to teach them to speak good English." We met a pastor who felt that part of his mission was to keep alive the Spanish language and the culture that it represents. We found churches where athletic games were going on outdoors while the women learned to cook and sew indoors. Underlying all programs of useful activities was the Christian appeal to the personal. Some churches express it in mass meetings and some through personal visitation and counseling, but all seek to exalt Jesus Christ as the one altogether worthy of the highest loyalty, the all-sufficient Saviour.

In evaluating the work of these social centers, Dr. Glenn W. Moore writes:

With older people not using the English language easily, with uncertain economic basis, with prejudice against Protestant churches, and with fear of persons prying into personal affairs, it is often difficult to establish contact with Mexican families. But a program of storytelling, of crafts, of games, and a friendly worker can soon establish confidence and friendship with children. Attitudes of cooperation, sociability, and confidence soon are developed. Christian workers can find many ways to tell the Christian story and awaken an interest.

The doors of homes otherwise closed are soon opened to the visitor who is a friend of the children in the household. Mothers are invited to visit the House of Neighborly Service and find help in their problems. A nurse helps when sickness comes. Soon many homes know that the House of Neighborly Service is a place of friendship and help. It is then found that this place exists because the people who operate it are Christians and are therefore interested in the welfare of the people of the neighborhood.

Some fine Christian homes may now be witnessed, established by young people first touched by the church in this way.

A church is found next to each House. The minister of at least one of these is himself the product of the House that he went to as a boy seeking companionship. Other former young people are now teachers, social workers, housewives, and elders in churches. Community Chests have recognized the value of the service and have supported these enterprises. This has been another way of ministering in the name of Christ.

When we approached the El Salvador Baptist Church, members of an interracial Mexican-Negro Sunday school were leaving the building. The advent of a housing project adjoining the church property had led the congregation to establish an English-speaking Sunday school in which the teachers were Mexicans but most of the pupils Negroes. Inside the church, we found that the regular Spanish-speaking Sunday school was still in session. The transition from it to the church service was not marked by anybody going out or coming in but by the superintendent leaving the platform and the pastor taking his place. It happened to be Fathers' Day. As part of the observance, all the fathers present, to the number of about twenty, were lined up across the front of the church and asked, first, how many children they had and, second, where they were. One father reported twelve and another eight and the rest less impressive figures. A few had some of their children with them; the rest reported that they were scattered from Korea to the Atlantic Coast. The atmosphere was informal and folksy; the congregation shared lustily in all of the proceedings. One could see how such a church service might compensate for a week of humble and not too much appreciated toil.

At another Mexican Baptist church, the service was more formal, although at one time all newcomers were asked what denomination they belonged to. The preaching was eloquent and the attention close. The first church was an expression of the group life; the second church was an agency for evangelizing men. Both are needed, and both are powerful. In both instances the people were present in good numbers.

In the Los Angeles area there are four notable Protestant institutions.

The Plaza Community Center stands at the heart of Old Los Angeles. Here the Spanish built their first adobe huts—a strange beginning for the present far-flung metropolis. In the years before the second world war this was the center of Japanese life. Today it is a strange mixture of old and new, a spot where all sorts and conditions of men meet and mingle. Facing the old square is the Plaza Community Center, which is first of all a Methodist church with 600 members drawn from all over the city and second a five-story, glistening white building dedicated to all manner of good works. It operates a clinic, employs a welfare worker, carries on many classes and much shop work, sends 80 boys and girls to camp every summer, and operates a children's home in Sierra Madre. The total budget is $56,000 a year, much of it drawn from home missionary sources. This is a dramatic Protestant approach to the Spanish-speaking Americans of the Southwest.

Mexican young people are offered the experience of living in a happy Christian atmosphere while attending school by other Methodist institutions, including the Spanish American Institute for boys at Gardena and the Frances DePauw School for girls, in Los Angeles. Both began as schools, but both now send their young people to the public schools, adding to this training a Christian home life and many extracurricular activities. The girls learn to keep house, to enjoy music, to teach English to those who need it, while the boys at Gardena look after sixty of the finest cows in the Los Angeles area. For hundreds of young people of Mexican parentage who have known little of well established homes, these institutions have opened the door upon a new way of living together.

Although located in East Los Angeles, the work and influence of the Spanish American Baptist Seminary extends far beyond California. It is the only college grade school for the training of ministers in continental United States in which Spanish is the language of instruction. In a recent year it enrolled students from California, Arizona, Missouri, Michigan, Illinois, Indiana, Kansas, and New York, not to mention Mexico, Puerto Rico, Guatemala, Cuba, and Colombia. Young women constitute about a fifth of the student body. Work is of college level, but with a five year course. The school is supported by the American Baptist Home Missionary Society.

Graduates of this seminary have gone out to serve faithfully and effectively wherever Spanish is spoken. Some have attained distinction as professors and writers. One of them is the present national director of the American Baptist Spanish work.

An international school such as this attracts unusual characters. One such, whose father was a prosperous business man in Mexico, left home at eighteen "to see the world," and was disinherited. After much wandering, he went to live with his sister in Tijuana, where she was a member of the Baptist church. She persuaded him to go with her to church, with the result that he was baptized. Shortly thereafter two Mexican Baptist ministers became martyrs at the hands of a mob. He decided to devote his life to taking the place of one of these men—and so he has made the strange transition from Tijuana to the Baptist Seminary in Los Angeles.

Almost as interesting is the story of another student at the seminary. He was born in Puerto Rico, the oldest of a large family. At the age of fourteen the family moved to New York city, where he became a member of the Second Spanish Baptist Church. He graduated from high school in New York. His mother has a good position, and he had every reason to believe that he could do well in business—but he felt a call to the ministry, and so he crossed the continent that he might learn to preach in the Spanish language.

Arizona is in many ways becoming an extension of southern California, as both citrus fruits and winter visitors bring increasing prosperity. It has the smallest Spanish-speaking population of any of the border states—and the least current immigration from Mexico. In general the picture is the same as for southern California, with the mines and the railroads as among the largest employers of Mexicans.

In Nogales, Arizona has the largest port of entry into Mexico west of El Paso, with Laredo, Texas, its only other rival as a gateway between the two nations. In Nogales has taken place one of the brightest stories of Christian service in the annals of modern home missions.

O. A. Smith started his ministry in the United Brethren Church in Michigan, but for reasons of health he found it necessary to move west, and in the process he became a Congregationalist. In 1920 he was sent to the little home missionary church in Nogales, and has been there ever since. In those days the international boundary line ran down the middle of a wide and dusty street that had one curb in Mexico and the other in the United States. This has since been replaced by a high wire fence through which one can peer from one country into the other. Mr. Smith arrived just as Mexico was subsiding into order after ten years of active revolution. Until the appointment of Dwight Morrow as ambassador to Mexico in 1927 the relations between the two countries were marked by mutual suspicions and ill will. During the decade of turmoil each had repeatedly exasperated the other. At the border this meant that all sorts of people got into all sorts of trouble with both governments.

Mr. Smith was concerned with people rather than with international relations. People sensed that his heart was good and that he might be their "friend in need." Both Americans and Mexicans sought him out with their various difficulties. His patience, his good sense, and his incorrigible smile enabled him to straighten matters out—especially as the officials on both sides of the line soon came to trust him. Under his leadership a social service bureau was set up to take care of the "situations" of human distress that were continually arising. This was financed locally, and for many years was headed by this home missionary pastor.

As the years have gone by, Nogales, Arizona, has had fewer and fewer Anglo citizens and more and more Mexican residents. Mr. Smith has continued to be everybody's friend, and is now pastor of the combined Congregational and Methodist churches, which makes him the one Protestant Anglo minister of the city. This important link in the international boundary is a more human, happier place because of his ministry. By way of recognition, some years ago the government of Mexico invited O. A. Smith, Protestant home missionary, to attend the inauguration of a president of the republic as its guest and at its expense. At Nogales, home missionary effort has achieved international recognition.

Many Protestant agencies sponsor work among Spanish-speaking people. To consolidate these efforts the Interdenominational Council on Spanish-speaking Work was organized in 1911. It is representative of both field workers and boards of missions. It has helped provide a community spirit among the Protestant churches serving Spanish-speaking people.

The council has fostered cooperative leadership training, religious education, and youth work. A strong program of women's work is sponsored by the General Department of United Church Women.

Should the council try to develop a strong group consciousness among Spanish-speaking churches, or should it lead toward the full integration of all Protestant work? To develop a strong group consciousness might bring a distinctiveness amounting to segregation. Integration might mean a needy field would be lost to sight. Here is an unsolved dilemma.

However, the council must continue to provide a channel for cooperation until Christian united fellowship becomes a reality.

Picking pecks of peppers is a back breaker as well as a tongue twister. This is "stoop" labor.

) CHAPTER 5 (

Mexicans on Wheels

ANCIENT jalopies with black haired, dark faced drivers and overloaded with both children and household goods have been a common sight on our Western highways. The most recent role of the Mexican on the American scene has been that of a migrant agricultural laborer flitting from crop to crop. In this capacity he has taken from the ground or plucked from the tree much food that has entered American mouths. He has also scattered himself far and wide over our country. In many places the visits of Mexican migrants have been the prelude to the establishment of a Mexican settlement.

Mexicans do not rattle about from place to place because they enjoy traveling. Their instincts are not at all nomadic. For boys even to think about running away from home is contrary to their traditions. Mexicans move about from necessity.

In this large-scale movement of Mexican workers there is both a push and a pull, with the former probably a bit stronger than the latter.

Two facts of life in Mexico explain both the source of this flood of humanity and the forces that have set it in motion. The population of Mexico has increased from 16.5 million in 1930 to 25.5 million in 1950, with a 30 per cent gain during the past decade. The simple fact is that the resources of the country have not expanded sufficiently to take care of the extra mouths to be fed. This basic situation has been further aggravated by inflation, which has been twice as severe as in this country. Taking 1939 as a base line (or 100) the cost of living in Mexico City was 354 by June of 1950, as compared with 171 in the United States for the same period.

Over against these facts should be put another. In 1949 the per capita income in the United States was $1,453; in Mexico it was $114. The greater the disparity of income and opportunity between the two sides of a boundary line, the greater the pressure to which that line will be exposed. Stories and pictures of the opulence of this country inspire the hungry, tattered Mexican with a great desire to push on across the line and help himself to some of our much advertised wealth.

But there is also a pull from this side. American agriculture, shifting to a large-scale mechanical operation, produces more food and fiber with relatively fewer workers. The year round employment of hired workers on our farms is decreasing. This same process has accentuated the need for part-time workers, particularly during the harvest. Plowing, planting, cultivating have been mechanized far more easily and quickly than cotton picking or the getting of sugar beets out of the ground. When it comes to the picking of cherries and strawberries, it would be hard to find anything to take the place of human fingers.

This situation has been aggravated by the long-time practice of using cheap labor for these processes. In some areas human hands are still cheaper than machines. As long as people can be had to work for little, the farmer is not likely to offer them more. But in recent years it has become increasingly difficult to enlist what is known as "stoop labor." The better wages offered in industry have drawn off many of those who once worked on farms. Why torture oneself bending over all day when more money can be had at jobs that are both less exhausting and much steadier? Inevitably farmers have turned their eyes southward across the border in their quest for cheap help. All along the boundary the argument is heard, "For many years we have had willing workers at a low wage from Mexico. Our farms have been developed on this basis. Are we not entitled to it now?"

Mexican migrant workers in this country fall into three groups: "wetbacks" who have entered the country illegally, contract workers brought in under an agreement between the two countries, and Mexicans who have become permanent and legal residents of this country. We will describe them in this order.

By common usage "wetback" means any Mexican who has gotten into the country without interviewing the immigration authorities. With the vast extent of the boundary, most of it running through very sparsely settled country, and with the very scant numbers of the border patrol, this is not a difficult matter. The term "wetback" is a fine sample of Western humor of the tall tale variety. Except in flood times, it is rarely necessary to get wet above the knees to cross the Rio Grande River.

As to the extent of this movement, the President's Commission on Migratory Labor reports:

The magnitude of the wetback traffic has reached entirely new levels in the past seven years. The number of deportations and voluntary departures has continuously mounted each year from 29,000 in 1944 to 565,000 in 1950. In its newly achieved proportions it is virtually an invasion. It is estimated that at least 400,000 of our migratory farm labor force of one million in 1949 were wetbacks.

The same report describes how this movement operates.

The hub of the wetback traffic is in the plazas of the Mexican towns and cities immediately below the border. Here, or in sections around the railroad which serve the same purpose, the wetback seeks information about jobs in the United States and how to get them. His urgent need of food and money makes him an easy mark for the smuggler, the labor contractor, or the agent of the farm employer. He is eager when any of these approach him and whisper that there is a way to get out of the vast mob, all looking for a job, and a chance to get into the United States where jobs seem plentiful and wages seem high.

Although the smuggling of wetbacks is widespread, the majority of wetbacks apparently enter alone or in small groups without a smuggler's assistance. In a group moving without the aid of a smuggler there usually is one who has made the trip before and who is willing to show the way. Not infrequently the same individual knows the farm to which the group intends to go and sometimes he has made advance arrangements with the farm employer to return at an appointed date with his group. Such wetbacks stream into the United States by the thousands through the deserts near El Paso and Calexico or across the Rio Grande between Rio Grande City and Brownsville. When employment on the farms adjacent to the border is filled, the wetbacks push northward into new areas following rumor or promise of employment.

Often the wetbacks entering alone or in small groups have written to farm employers or friends and have made arrangements to be met at some crossroad, gate, or other well known place within a night's walk of the border. Some make two or three separate entries within a season, after having been apprehended, and head for the place where they were formerly employed.

If the wetback makes a deal to be guided or escorted across the Rio Grande or some section of the land border, everything which he is able to pay is usually extracted from him in return for the service, which may be no more than being guided around the fence or being given a boat ride across the Rio Grande. Wetbacks who are without funds to pay the smuggler for bringing them in or to pay the trucker-contractor who furnishes transportation or direction from the boundary to the farm are frequently "sold" from one exploiter to the next. For example, the smuggler will offer to bring a specified number of wetbacks across the river for such an amount as $10 or $15 per man. The smuggler or boatman with his party in tow will be met by the trucker-contractor who will then "buy" the wetback party by paying off the smuggler. This trucker-contractor, in turn, will have a deal to deliver workers to employers at an agreed-upon price per head.

Once on the United States side of the border and on the farm, numerous devices are employed to keep the wetback on the job. Basic to these devices is the fact that the wetback is a person of legal disability who is under jeopardy of immediate deportation if caught. He is told that if he leaves the farm, he will be reported to the Immigration Service or that, equally unfortunate for him, the Immigration Service will surely find him if he ventures into town or out onto the roads. To assure that he will stay until his services are no longer needed, his pay, or some portion thereof, frequently is held back. Sometimes he is deliberately kept indebted to the farmer's store or commissary until the end of the season, at which time he may be given enough to buy shoes or clothing and encouraged to return the following season.

The wetback is a hungry human being. His need of food and clothing is immediate and pressing. He is a fugitive and it is as a fugitive that he lives. Under the constant threat of apprehension and deportation, he cannot protest or appeal no matter how unjustly he is treated. Law operates against him but not for him. Those who capitalize on the legal disability of the wetbacks are numerous and their devices are many and various.

During the last two or three years the wetback has received much publicity, and efforts have been made by the government and others to have something effective done about his plight, but as yet the results have been meager. Deportation is often futile, as he comes back in a day or two. It is said that the Immigration Service tried flying repatriated wetbacks far into Mexico, but that they return just the same. The man who profits by the wetback is his employer, and as yet no real penalties have been invoked against him.

Inevitably such a fly-by-night person as the wetback can have little contact with churches, either Roman Catholic or Protestant. He may be in the United States for some months, but he is not of it. The effect of the wetback upon the position of his fellow Mexicans in this country will be discussed in connection with the other phases of agricultural migrancy.

A second group of migrant workers are the Mexicans brought into the United States under contract on the basis of an agreement between our government and that of Mexico. This arrangement began during the first world war as an emergency measure to assure help in harvesting. Between 1917 and 1921, 73,000 Mexicans were brought into this country on a temporary basis. This practice was revived in 1943 and extended to include workers from Jamaica, the Bahama Islands, and elsewhere. Between 1942 and 1947 our government brought 219,500 Mexicans into this country at public expense. The agreement with Mexico has been repeatedly extended, with the result that over 100,000 Mexicans were imported in 1949 and just over 90,000 in 1950.

To secure Mexicans under contract, it is necessary for farmers to certify that they are unable to obtain the labor needed from American sources and to agree to pay the prevailing wage to these workers, as well as to meet certain other conditions that we will mention later. Necessarily this statement of need must be filed some time before the harvest, and therefore is somewhat hypothetical. The most that the farmer can do is to state that he "expects" a shortage. Harvests are at best brief. The farmer wants to have enough workers on hand to get the crop gathered in a short period of time. His view of what constitutes a shortage is quite different from that of the workers.

The prevailing wage is also somewhat hypothetical. At the beginning of the season the farmers set a figure at which they hope they can secure sufficient workers to serve their ends. If workers prove scarce, this figure may be boosted. The effect of importing Mexicans is to make labor abundant and thus to make the prevailing wage rather less than would have been the case if it had been necessary for the farmers to bid for workers from a lesser number of possible harvesters.

On the other hand, the Mexicans who come in under contract enjoy certain advantages that are denied to American workers—such as health care, a reasonable standard for both the transportation and the housing provided them, and the assurance that they will be returned to the place where they started. In case the terms of the agreement are violated by the employer, the employee has the privilege of appealing to the Mexican consul. During his employment the Mexican under contract has a security that those who live here all year do not know.

Both the wetbacks and the Mexicans under contract are resented by the migratory workers who have permanent residence in this country —both those of American and those of Mexican descent. They feel that citizens of this country should have the same guarantees that are given to aliens. More important, they feel that the ability of the farmers to secure both illegal and contract labor has enabled them to keep wages at a lower level than would otherwise have been the case. This is substantiated by the President's Commission on Migratory Labor, which states bluntly, "We find that alien labor has depressed farm wages and, therefore, has been detrimental to domestic labor."

In the early months of 1943 the writer visited a number of the migrant labor camps that were being maintained at that time by the government in Florida and Texas. The men in charge of these camps did not believe that there was any need for the importation of alien labor but that with proper adjustments as to wages, period of work, and housing accommodations enough laborers could be found in this country to take care of agricultural needs. The President's Commission is of the same mind. It reports:

Since 1945 more hired workers are being employed to do continuously less work. Many imperfections in the employment structure of American agriculture result in poor use of our labor resources. Notwithstanding these imperfections and obstacles to effective use of labor, we are convinced that, by the better recruitment and placement of domestic labor, we would have eliminated most if not all the occasion for the certifications of labor shortage during the years 1947 to 1950.

That is, if American agriculture attacked this problem with energy, resourcefulness, and ingenuity, we could get along without either the wetbacks or the legally imported labor of Mexico—and our agricultural workers would be better off.

The President's Commission states the matter rather poignantly:

> Migrants are children of misfortune. They are the rejects of those sectors of agriculture and of other industries undergoing change. We depend upon misfortune to build up our force of migratory workers and when the supply is low because there is not enough misfortune at home, we rely on misfortune abroad to replenish the supply.

During the war years, Mexico refused to send contract labor to Texas because of the discriminations practiced against Mexicans, with the result that most of the legally imported workers during that period went to California and the Pacific Northwest. Since the war, Mexico has lifted the ban against Texas, with the result that in recent years most of the contract labor has gone to Texas, New Mexico, and Arkansas. Although these men (no families are brought in under contract) have been relatively well cared for, they have had few real contacts with American life, particularly the churches.

We now come to the third group—the Mexicans who came to this country legally and who regard themselves as permanent residents.

It should be stressed that this is not too difficult a status to attain. Unlike most parts of the world, Mexico does not have an immigration quota. There are no limits to the number who may be legally admitted to residence in the United States during a given year. The barriers, such as they are, are administrative and technical. Any reasonably persistent Mexican who is not afraid of paper work can secure admission.

Such an immigrant needs to secure permission from the Mexican Government to leave and permission from a United States consul to enter. He must meet the requirements as to health and moral character. He must either produce one hundred dollars in cash at the border or have letters promising support from friends or relatives already in the country. To get a friend in, a Mexican living in this country needs such things as letters from his banker and employer, possibly from some church, a tax receipt if possible, and so on. These are undoubtedly burdensome requirements to unlettered people, but they are not impossible.

There is another and rather interesting way that a Mexican can stay in this country, or even return to it. Every child born in this country whose parents do not claim citizenship for him elsewhere is by that very fact a citizen of the United States. Except when they come in as contract laborers. Mexicans commonly bring their families with them— and frequently give birth to American citizens. Any baby for whom somebody will claim the right can stay in the United States or even return to it. Now to separate a baby or a small child from its parents would cause distress to all concerned. To prevent such distress any Mexicans who can prove that their child was born beneath our flag can remain in the United States. After a person has resided here legally for seven years he achieves the "right of residence" and cannot ordinarily be deported. Thus it is far easier for Mexicans to enter the United States legally than for people of most of the other nations. However, we have a suspicion that the person who can meet the requirements for residence is not the sort of person who is likely to become a migrant agricultural worker after he gets here.

It is plain hunger that brings the Mexican farm worker into the United States either legally or illegally. It is his inability to earn a living in one place that compels the American of Mexican descent to take to the road, as shown by the following testimony before the Senate sub-committee on migratory farm labor:

My name is Jacinto Cota, Jr. I do all kinds of farm work in the fields. Right now I am loading carrots. All my life I have lived in the Imperial Valley. All my friends and I have worked with the wetbacks and the nationals and we know these conditions that we are talking about. They have pushed out our local people because they will do any kind of work on farms for low wages. The ranchers tell them in old Mexico that they are going to get different good wages. They promise good houses. . . . The labor contractors gyp the nationals. They make them pay high prices for food, blankets, and medicine. All the local people will have to leave the valley if they keep bringing in nationals and wetbacks.

Obviously few Mexicans who have established themselves on this side of the border voluntarily choose to become migrants. The hunger and want of Mexico pushes her people across the international boundary and deprives those already here of at least a part of their employment. In order to maintain the standard of living they have attained, they take to the road. Here they find life unsatisfactory for many reasons, chief of which are irregular employment and low wages.

According to a survey made by the United States Department of Agriculture, in 1949 the average migratory farm worker got 70 days of farm work and 31 days of non-farm work, making a total for the year of 101 days with annual earnings averaging $514. These figures included everybody over fourteen years of age for both sexes. Almost a third of the workers were women, while between one-fourth and one-fifth of the workers were between the ages of fourteen and seventeen. Everybody must help. The larger the family, the larger the income, but even then two thousand dollars a year is unusual. On the other hand, for the actual time they work migratory workers make a little more than non-migratory workers—but this is more than offset by the irregularity of their employment and the cost of getting around.

The President's Commission reports:

Although migratory farm workers travel long distances to get employment, very few of them use the bus or train. In the ordinary sense of the
word, they do not travel; most of them are hauled.

Whether supplied by contractors or employers, the trucks used too frequently are old and dilapidated and generally unfit for carrying people.
There have been many accidents which would not have happened had the
driver not been exhausted from continuous driving or if the truck had been
in proper mechanical repair. In many cases no rest stops are made though
the trip requires thirty-six hours or more. One reason why trucks come
straight through from points of origin to points of destination is that there
are no accommodations for rest stops en route. A survey in Indiana reveals
that the most frequent suggestion of workers from Texas was the need for
"rest camps along the route at which they might stop to clean up, rest, and
cook."

At this point Mexican contract workers fare better than American
citizens:

The Mexican worker's contract provides for transportation by common
carrier or in approved equipment. Conditions which must be met include:
insurance to protect the workers against injury en route; fixed seats and
covering against inclement weather; hours of travel limited to twelve per
day, not to commence before four A. M. and not to continue after eight P. M.;
ten minute rest stops every two hours with half hour stops for meals;
provision of overnight accommodation; an experienced, licensed driver who
agrees to observe the safety regulations of common carriers.

Next to modes of travel, the housing or lack thereof is the greatest
hardship for migratory workers. The shorter their stay, the scantier
the provision for their needs. The President's Commission states:

On job, housing consists of barracks, cabins, trailers, tents, rooming
houses, auto-court cabins, shack houses, and depreciated standard housing.
Ownership may be by employers' associations, local housing authorities,
labor contractors, or private commercial groups.

"Good" housing for a family of four, five, or six members might consist of an unpainted cabin, 9 by 12 feet, one in a row of such cabins, with one or perhaps two screened windows (though not necessarily with glass) and with unfinished interior walls. The cabin would be equipped with bunks, chairs, and table. It would be fairly clean and free from vermin. The cabin might possibly, but probably would not, have electricity. It could have running water, but this would be unusual. Characteristically, water suitable for drinking would be obtained from centrally located faucets. Cooking facilities, if existent, would probably be central. (We have seen a dozen stoves, each assigned to a different family, all in one big room.) Sanitary facilities would be central and clean. In exceptional cases, there would be flush toilets; more often, there would be privies. Central shower facilities would be equipped with hot and cold water. In the better camps there would be facilities for laundering and receptacles for garbage which would be regularly emptied. There would probably be no trees about the cabins, so that during the summer months they would be fully exposed to the sun.

To be "good" a camp is not required to have any provisions for recreation, but it might be located within walking distance of a community center. If, by chance, a school was nearby, the children could attend. If it was not so located, no alternative arrangements would be made for schooling. No arrangements would exist for the care of the small children. Since both parents often work, the children would be left to their own devices or would join their parents in the field. If, as is usual, the camp is located beyond the reach of medical and health facilities, it would be unusual if arrangements existed for regular visits of a nurse or physician.

A series of such "good" camps, or a single such camp, might, if the migrant were fortunate, be his home for four to six months of the year. If so, he would be one of a minority, because even in those states that officially inspect and rate their camps, less than one half of the inspected camps are found to be "good."

The work of the migrant is terribly impersonal. He rarely sees and hardly ever knows his employer. He is a "hand" rather than a human being, and works for a crop rather than a person. This is reflected in his use of words. He works "in cotton," "in beets," "in carrots," "in cherries." His labor is wholly without personal recognition. Often no payroll is kept; the worker brings in the fruit or vegetables or cotton that he has picked and is paid for his work by the basket or other container.

Mexican migrants have two points of departure: southern California and Texas.

The "swing" of the Mexican migrants in California is relatively short, with a range of about 500 miles. However, the work is remarkably varied, as shown by testimony before the President's Commission:

We start about in late April. The Valencia orange season starts in Tulare County. That lasts pretty well, usually up until June. Around the first of July, I leave there and go to the Sacramento River and work in the pear houses. The pear harvest in that area is the first pears that ripen in California. That usually lasts about three weeks. There is usually also a time right in there in Lake County—a week or so—and then pears start in other places —Tulare County, Santa Clara County. The pear harvest will last pretty well into September, and then the walnuts start. And then I return home in October, and the olive crop is about to start. Early in November we have another orange crop season. That usually carries through until the middle of January.

With the exception of "some little pruning in citrus and grapes in March" the witness usually has no work from mid-January to late April. He reported his earnings for the year to be between $1,800 and $2,000.

The Texas-Mexicans are a more traveled lot. In our chapter on Texas we told how they follow the cotton crop within the state. There is also the great migration from the Rio Grande Valley and San Antonio to the Yakima Valley in Washington for apples and hops, to Montana, Colorado, Nebraska, and Kansas for sugar beets, and to central Michigan for sugar beets and fruits. A glance at the map will show that the distances involved are terrific.

Sugar beets are the crop most intimately associated with Mexicans— probably because it involves really violent labor. In Montana I have

Top, Division of Foreign Missions, NCCC; *bottom*, Ray Draper

seen a Mexican girl who could hardly have been twenty years old pull beets out of the ground, knock them together to shake off the dirt, and toss them to one side at a speed that made picture taking most difficult. In Michigan I have seen Mexican men swishing off the tops of beets with a rapidity that taxed the eye. This is exhausting work—and yet the Mexicans manage to stick at it for hours.

In the western areas German-speaking immigrants from Russia were the original beet workers. At the opening of the century they did the work that the Mexicans now do; today they "own the beets." Will the Mexicans follow their example? It is not impossible.

Some years back stories were current of non-stop "standing room only" truck rides for Mexicans from San Antonio to the area north of Lansing, Michigan, but we believe that this is of the past. In its handling of migrant labor, Michigan has led the other states. Before he leaves Texas, the worker is commonly given both a medical examination and a contract. Also the growers in Michigan have gone further than elsewhere in providing continuous employment by shifting the workers around from crop to crop and place to place. Between the thinning and the harvesting of the sugar beets, employment may be had in cherries or peas, or the workers may be shipped to Wisconsin or even Minnesota, at the employers' expense, to assist in crops there. Michigan is fortunate in having a variety of fruit and vegetable crops, often in the same areas, but it has also demonstrated what can be done when an effort is made to provide continuous employment even in the face of seasonal conditions.

There are reasons to believe that the Mexicans who have permanently established themselves in this country will become less migratory as the years go by.

Mechanization is taking place in the two crops that have employed the largest numbers of migrants: cotton and sugar beets.

The rise of the cotton picking machine is shown by these figures from the San Joaquin Valley, where cotton is a major crop. In 1945 less than one per cent of the crop was picked by machines, but by 1949, 17 per cent was handled in this way, with a 1950 estimate of 35 per cent and with a lively expectation that very shortly 90 per cent of the crop will be gathered mechanically.

From the Arizona Cotton Cooperative Growers' Association comes some interesting testimony:

> We believe that we can see the time in the very near future when cotton picking machines will eliminate most of the problems caused by migrant labor in Arizona. At the present time we have in the state enough machines to pick approximately 25 per cent of the crop if they are used full time. The machines must have skillful operators, and they cannot be trained overnight. They are taking over the biggest part of the total. The grower will gain more economical harvesting of his cotton at a time when he wants to do it, making it unnecessary for him to worry much about the labor supply. However, machines will never replace all of the labor. Early in the season cotton must be picked by hand.

The mechanization of the sugar beet harvest is already far advanced in California, where between 85 and 90 per cent of the work is now done by machines. Michigan is less advanced but is on its way. The work of thinning the beets remains, but this is being reduced by changes in the seeds and in better planting practices. A mechanical beet thinner has been proved practical and may soon be on the market. Apparently it is only a matter of time until the human back and the human arm will be excused from the arduous task of getting sugar beets out of the ground.

Progress is in prospect on other fronts. A spokesman for the California citrus fruit industry has stated, "We have in the research laboratories machines which will eventually take care of the need for additional labor in the citrus industry. Given another three or four years, assuming we can go along using the inventive skill that we have, I don't think that the citrus industry will be in need of migrant labor."

There is even hope for such a tender thing as asparagus. Two years ago the secretary of the California Asparagus Growers' Association said, "We have a machine in the field this year. It is the second year of research into the development of mechanical harvesting. We feel that eventually we will develop a harvester that will handle the harvesting of asparagus."

This does not mean that the need for migratory workers will disappear overnight. The day when cherries, strawberries, blueberries, peaches, and other fruits will be picked by machines is not imminent. But increasingly the hardest tasks will be done mechanically rather than by human muscles. It is also true that the higher the wage paid for human energy, and the better the care required for human machines, the more rapidly will they be superseded. On the other hand, the cheaper the labor available, the less the enthusiasm for machines. Mechanization is not a live issue in those areas where wetbacks can be had. Agriculture is not immune from the principle that has made American industry great: the higher wages go, the greater the incentive to devise machines to do the work.

A second reason why we may expect migrancy among Mexicans to decline is their own desire to settle down. No group has ever remained permanently migratory. Mexicans will grasp at any straw that promises them permanency. When they get to a place where there is a good roof over their heads, they do their best to stay. The farmers and farming communities are anxious that the people who gather their crops should go back to where they came from as soon as the harvest is over. One of the attractions of the wetbacks and the Mexican contract workers is that they are easy to get rid of.

An interesting development is that wherever Mexicans have been, a permanent settlement of Mexicans usually grows up. In spite of the anonymity of their work and the impersonal nature of their employment, here and there a Mexican will sell himself to the boss as a good worker who might be a year around asset. They have considerable skill in managing irrigation. Many of them have "green fingers" when it comes to handling growing plants. They have brains as well as brawn—and terrific energy when they see a chance to better themselves. In our next chapter we will discuss these clusters of Mexicans scattered about the country, which may prove to be the finest fruit of their toilsome years as agricultural migrants.

The religious organization most successful in making contacts with Mexican migratory workers has been the Division of Home Missions of the National Council of Churches.

About thirty years ago the former Council of Women for Home Missions discovered the agricultural migrants. Their hearts were touched by the plight of these workers, and they undertook to do something about it. This began by employing young women to tend the babies while their mothers worked in the fields—a task of almost pure humanitarianism. Out of these nurseries came centers that gradually provided the equivalent of Daily Vacation Bible Schools for the older children, recreation for the young people, some measure of health care for everybody, and, in some instances, religious services. In addition to college students of both sexes, venturesome schoolteachers were employed for the vacation period, with finally a year-around staff who followed the migrants from the Rio Grande Valley to Minnesota and Michigan, by way of the strawberry patches of Louisiana and Arkansas. In the early years, the migrants served were largely of Anglo-Saxon ancestry, but recently more attention has been paid to the Negroes and the Mexicans. Ordained ministers from both groups have been employed for full-time work among their people.

This Protestant agency has had contacts with Mexican migrants in California, the Rio Grande Valley, and elsewhere in Texas, Arizona, Colorado, Minnesota, and Michigan. Its efforts have been twofold: to serve the needs of these people but at the same time to lead the communities in which they labor to accept some responsibility for them. This has begun with local financial support for the centers but has developed into cooperation in the use of schools and churches and some community contacts with the Mexicans. The ultimate aim is to have the Mexicans recognized as human beings rather than as a cheap substitute for machines. The amount of religious instruction has varied with circumstances. The Okies and Arkies and the Negroes are far readier to attend religious services than are the Mexicans, both for reasons of language and because of their traditions.

The migrant centers have reached their highest development in Michigan, thanks to the cooperation of state and county councils of churches and, in some instances, of the school authorities. A large degree of financial responsibility has been accepted locally. In some instances, the women of the neighboring churches take turns in supplying the noon lunch. Vacation schools and local church groups visit the centers and join in games with the migrant children. Unused schoolhouses, and some that are modern and regularly used, have been made available for migrant centers.

I visited a lovely example of community cooperation at Mt. Pleasant, Michigan, where the State Teachers' College was operating an experimental summer school for both English-speaking and Mexican children. The equipment was that of a model school. The children came equally from the two groups. They were playing together, doing art work together, and studying both English and Spanish together, with teachers of both national backgrounds. The Home Missions Council—as it was then called—was cooperating by assigning a worker to visit in the Mexican homes to interpret the school and encourage the children's attendance.

Probably the greatest service that organized Protestantism has rendered the agricultural migrants has been to publicize them and their needs. Before the appearance of *The Grapes of Wrath*, the American people were hardly aware of their existence. It was the women of the churches who got the word "migrant" into the language. It was the pioneering of the church that stirred the state to action.

Today the Western Area of the Division of Home Missions has a year-around staff of eight working with agricultural migrants, most of whom are Mexicans. This is supplemented with a considerable number of college students, who may be supported by their denominations, their local churches, or work on a volunteer basis. Here are some of their reports for the summer of 1952:

From Colorado: The summer program began in mid-June with the arrival of the summer staff for the two-day Training Institute. With excellent crops all over Colorado, many migratory workers were used, including 200-300 Navajo Indians on the Western Slope; several hundred Spanish Americans, Sioux Indians, and Mexicans in the Arkansas Valley, and scattered families in the San Luis Valley and northern Colorado.

The special unit of study was the Christian Home and Family Life, chosen by the staff and offering an excellent opportunity to get acquainted with families and the children. Before many days the community center took on a new look with pictures, scrapbooks, spatter prints, miniature houses, cutouts of family groups, and dioramas of homes of many lands.

Fun Night brought folks from all directions to Palisade, some to take part, some to watch. The highlight at Fort Lupton was the two performances for parents and friends staged by the children. One was a portrayal in a succession of tableaux of nursery rhymes while the other was the Parade of the Months. The children were simply thrilled at the thought of dressing up and going behind the footlights. The teachers struggled and sweat. They felt that they had both lost and won—lost a perfect production, but won a memorable experience for the children. Just try to keep excited, eager children from peering over the backdrop to see every other child take his part, and you will understand!

From Washington: The Mobile Chapel on Wheels has again been visiting the migrant camps. The children look forward to the beginning of the vacation schools, and the time of departure to a new camp brings with it some rather sorrowful good-bys.

The visual aid equipment and the portable organ make even more attractive and effective the work of the Chapel on Wheels. And these wheels roll a good many thousand miles during the course of a season, for reliable statistics indicate that this year there were over 21,000 migrant laborers in the state, not including members of the family who did not work.

Edith Mason, a summer worker, reports: The missionary story had come to an end. Immediately the picture of little children of various races gathered around the friendly figure of Jesus became the center of attraction. "Teacher, is it really like belonging to one family?" a child asked.

Before the teacher could answer, a five-year-old piped up, "In God's way it is."

Among the little children of this camp that phrase soon became a common expression. "We mustn't fight—in God's way we're all brothers and sisters."

"Let's ask Estrellita to come to our Bible school, too. In God's way she is our sister." Estrellita belonged to a new family that had just moved into the camp and she spoke a different language and her skin was a different color.

How different was the attitude of the schools nearby, where the migrant children were made to feel unwanted. How different was the attitude of the town toward the teenagers and the young people, where they were discriminated against because of their address.

Godliness and cleanliness go together, as revealed in this report: The child was bathing. Not in a big enamel bathtub, but in a wash tray in the camp laundry house. Not in hot, soapy water, but in cold water. It was all she had.

A staff member asked why she was taking a bath in the middle of the day. The child replied in Spanish, "I like to be clean because God loves clean children better than dirty ones, and I want him to love me. You and the other girls are always clean and neat, and I want to look pretty, too."

Opal Beymer, a staff member in California, writes: Those of us who stay on through the winter months get intimations of what our work has meant to the boys and girls.

There was eight-year-old Rachel who was in one of those out-of-the-way winter cotton camps. When the staff worker introduced a new song, she suddenly clapped her hands and danced all over the tent floor. "I know that song!" she cried with delight. "I learned it from my teacher when we were in Merced in the figs."

Eleven-year-old Mary—also in a winter camp—told over and over about the good times she had enjoyed in the summer school in a fruit camp where she had lived two summers before. Lovingly she brought out some of the articles that she had made and had carefully kept for two years.

Billy one day taught the group how to play a new game that "we learned when we were in a camp in Oregon."

Katherine Schaeffer, a summer camp worker, composed what she calls "A Migrant Mother's Prayer":

> Lord, give us a house that's clean and neat,
> And a refrigerator to keep our meat;
> A small fenced yard with grass so green,
> With children playing nice and clean.
>
> A little house in town, dear Lord,
> Where we may shop at a neighborhood store;
> And have close friends on either side
> And never have to say good-by.
>
> A place where we'll be welcomed
> By friends that we will make—
> At church, at school, at play, dear Lord,
> I pray for my children's sake.
>
> Just a little house, dear Lord,
> With pictures on the wall;
> And help us grow in Christian love,
> And happiness for all.

Miss Edith Lowry, executive secretary of the Division of Home Missions, sums up the interdenominational service to migrants that she directs by saying, "We want people to think of the migrant not as a problem, but as a person. In any situation we enter, we try to build cooperation and reconcile tension, rather than going in as a pressure group."

An observer comments, "This approach probably accounts for their success. For both growers and processors, on the one hand, and migrants, on the other, are likely to receive the division's first overtures with considerable skepticism. The grower or processor has the job of harvesting X tons of crops for Y dollars, and is afraid the division's efforts will alter this ratio."[1]

The home mission workers with migrants seek to reconcile the laborers and their families with one another and with God. There is also the job of building understanding and appreciation between employers and the labor force. Christian hope may be born, children and adults may be started on the path of education, but one thing more must be done. To save migrants from being itinerant strangers, someone must bridge the gap between them and the communities they visit. This, too, is the work of the Division of Home Missions, aided by local churches sensitive to the opportunity to practice Christianity in human relations.

The agricultural migrations of Mexicans in this country are probably passing their peak. Movements are on foot that will severely limit if not outlaw the wetback traffic. When that is stopped, there will be less occasion for the importation of Mexicans under contract, in part because the "prevailing wage" will then rise. Ultimately the employers of migrant labor will be compelled by economic necessity to do two things: to use the available labor more intelligently and economically, as is being done in Michigan and other Northern states at present, and to substitute machinery for men in the more arduous and backbreaking tasks.

Undoubtedly some will ask the questions: Will not the wetbacks get even hungrier if they are kept out of this country? What will happen to those legally here when they are displaced by machines?

To this there are several answers. The more fundamental one is that

[1] "The Ladies Had an Answer," by Paul Marcus, in *The Saturday Evening Post,* October 4, 1952. Used by permission.

we are never doing people a favor by employing them at starvation wages. Just keeping people alive is no help to progress, but impedes it. The Mexican Government is aware of this and has little enthusiasm for this traffic. Mexico's problem of poverty cannot be solved by sending workers across the border to lower the standards of those already here.

The sweatshop situation in this country at the beginning of the century is a close parallel to the one that we are discussing. The employment of men, women, and children for long hours under unsanitary conditions at miserable wages was abolished. What became of the victims of this situation? They did not starve; when they had to, they found something better to do. Neither did their employers go broke. With much machinery, good working conditions, and high wages the garment industry is in far better shape than it was fifty years ago. Much the same future can be expected for the Mexican migrants and the men who employ them. If they will apply the same intelligence to their problems that industry has done, American agriculture can be transformed into a self-respecting and profitable activity for both the workers and the owners. As for the Mexicans, they can evolve a better solution to their problems than rushing from crop to crop to earn a pittance.

Indirectly migratory labor has rendered the Mexicans a real service by distributing them over the country in a fashion that would probably have been impossible without it. If they are to live in the United States, they should become a part of our national life. As long as the Mexicans are massed along the Rio Grande Valley and in the Imperial Valley and similar sections of California their adjustment to American life is bound to be partial. Both their language and their employment encourages them to keep to themselves. The experience of other immigrant groups is that it is only as they scatter out that they become a true part of the American scene. How their experience as migrants has opened many doors of opportunity to them will be the theme of our next chapter.

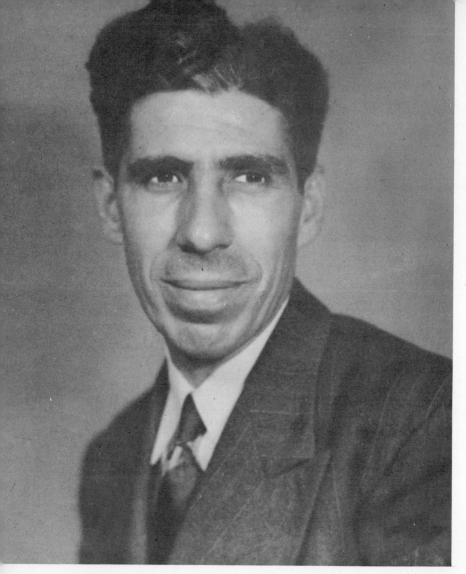

Brooke Baldwin

With hopeful persistence, Mexicans are establishing little beachheads in hundreds of communities.

) CHAPTER 6 (

Mexican Beachheads in the North

THE SECOND world war taught the American people that beachheads are difficult to establish and precarious to hold; that of and in themselves they do not amount to much, but if properly exploited they can lead almost anywhere.

Scattered across our country are little clumps of Mexicans who help to open doors into American life for their fellow countrymen. Their experience parallels that of soldiers landing on an alien shore. For soldiers, the first night is the worst; for the Mexican the first winter. It takes courage for a family to face the prospect of cold and snow for the first time, and usually with inadequate shelter. At the next point our analogy falls down. A military expeditionary force gets too much attention; a new Mexican family in town probably gets too little. They are rarely esteemed to be important. They are neither welcomed nor rebuffed because of their obvious harmlessness. But if a Mexican family remains in a community, it is almost certain to increase, both biologically and by the arrival of relatives and friends. As the children grow up and go to school, the way will finally open for them to become a part of the community.

In most Western and Northern communities this is far in the future. Usually the well-to-do element hardly know that their Mexican neighbors exist. We asked an intelligent and socially conscious minister who had served for nine years in a Montana sugar beet town what contacts and experiences he had had with the Mexicans who lived there. He looked blank and then replied, "None whatever." We suspect that he is quite typical.

Three types of employment have led to the establishment of Mexican settlements away from the border: the railroads, sugar beets, and steel.

In much of the West the Mexican laborer has inherited the pick and shovel with which first the Irish and then a long succession of European immigrants have done the necessary track work for our railroads. During the second world war, it was the Mexicans who kept our transcontinental lines in operation.

From the nature of the case the railroads distribute their employees widely. The remarkable feature of the Mexicans is the way they keep out of sight. The only time the traveler notices them is when he sees a string of freight cars marked "Maintenance of Way" and obviously overflowing with inhabitants sequestered on some siding. This is the first step, and obviously a transient one. The next is a house near the railroad, which may be its property and therefore is painted in its proprietary colors. As the prosperity of the Mexican increases, he acquires a better home.

The Mexicans have their share of bright boys, and some of them are bound to rise in the world. From the fixing of the track on which the trains run it is not too great a step to tinkering with the engines that pull the trains. In Gallup, New Mexico, we were told that a man of

Spanish-speaking ancestry was foreman of the roundhouse, and we heard of a similar instance elsewhere. From their humble position beside the tracks the children of these track men will both move into town and make their way upward in the railroad hierarchy, probably on the mechanical side to begin with.

As we have seen, it was originally expected that the Mexicans who came north to cultivate and pull the sugar beets would all be back in Texas by Hallowe'en at least. Apparently somebody usually managed to miss the return trip. Wherever you find beets, you find year-around Mexicans. The first step was to spend the winter in the barracks that the sugar company had built for what is locally known as "the campaign"—when the beets come out of the ground and are transformed into sugar. From the company houses they branched out into something a bit better for themselves. This has been the story in Montana, Colorado, Nebraska, Kansas, Iowa, Minnesota, and other states. The Mexicans live unobtrusively somewhere near the sugar factory. Their children go to school, and speak the English language habitually. A public health nurse in Montana told me that she found the Mexicans most cooperative. Nowhere have I heard complaints about them. They may not be accepted, but neither are they rejected.

In Michigan the pattern is somewhat different. Here the Mexicans have worked in various fruits as well as beets. Instead of clustering around the sugar beet refineries, the Mexicans have had their first homes on farms and then moved into town. Also, Michigan has many small and some large cities that have been growing rapidly in recent years and have attracted Mexicans. There appears to be considerable traffic back and forth between the cities and the harvest fields. We once encountered a Mexican who claimed to be a meat cutter in Muskegon, giving himself and his wife a bit of variety with a few weeks in the beets. In the summer of 1952 some forty or more Mexican families who were thrown out of work in Detroit by the steel strike improved their enforced vacation by going to the country to pick cherries.

Denver owes her 20,000 or more people of Spanish-speaking ancestry to two sources: beet workers moving to town, old Spanish working north from the plaza towns of New Mexico. The Mexican consul stated that there were only 1,500 Mexican citizens in the city—and that he could do nothing about the troubles in which American-born or naturalized Mexicans might become involved. He thought that there was some discrimination against Mexicans in Denver but that conditions were better than in many other places.

Many lines of employment seem to be open to Spanish-speaking people in Denver. Although a majority are laborers, there are also stenographers, clerks, teachers, and professional people. As seemed to be true in all cities, the Spanish-speaking people are spreading out. Once most of them had lived in the quite undesirable area north of the business center, but now many of them are moving to the west, which is "on the other side of the tracks," but which is nevertheless a moderately attractive residential area in which there is a considerable Jewish element. Bethel Presbyterian Church, which is Spanish-speaking, has recently moved into this area but reports no opposition whatever from its Jewish and other neighbors.

Conrad Pyle, boys' worker on the staff of the Epworth Methodist Church, which serves a mixed parish in connection with the Good Will Industries, reported that he had found the Spanish-speaking boys entirely trustworthy and that he had never seen anything that looked like a gang fight, although the boys regarded it as a matter of personal pride to hit back whenever anyone hit them. Somewhat less than half of his boys attend parochial grammar schools, but they all go to public high schools. After that the emphasis is on getting a job.

Spanish-speaking Protestants in Denver number approximately 2,000.

Three well established churches serve them. The Presbyterians have a new church in a good neighborhood, as we have mentioned, and also a House of Neighborly Service in the old Spanish section. There are Baptist churches and a community center here also.

The First Spanish Methodist Church has a prominent location about a mile from the business section. The building is an ancient monument to the piety of the eighteen-eighties that was assigned to a Spanish-speaking congregation during the twenties. Worship services and the church school are held on the ground floor; what was once the church proper now serves for basketball and dinners. The congregation once numbered 700 members, but during the depression half of these people either went back to Mexico or moved elsewhere, and the present membership is a little under four hundred.

The pastor, Hector Franco, was born in Mexico City and baptized a Roman Catholic. His father was an army man, his mother died when he was quite young, and so the three children of the family were sent to El Paso for safety. There he attended the Lydia Patterson Institute and later graduated from the Harwood Boys' School in Albuquerque. While attending these schools he was converted and began to study for the ministry. He has served six Spanish-speaking churches, and in each of them his people had a different type of employment. In Emporia, Kansas, they were railroad workers; in Lyons, Kansas, they toiled in the salt mines; in Garden City, Kansas, they worked "in beets"; in Kansas City, Kansas, they were employed in the railroad roundhouses and in the packing plants; in Wichita, Kansas, they did "city work," which means personal service with some store and office jobs, and were also employed at the Boeing airplane plant; in Denver it was "city work" again. He said, "The more our people are in a minority, the greater are the opportunities for the individual to branch out in new lines of work and to get ahead generally."

The third movement of Mexicans to the North and East is industrial, and quite different from the other two that we have described. Both as railroad workers and as agricultural migrants the Mexicans were employed as groups rather than as individuals. They came in numbers, ordinarily bringing their families with them. They lived apart from the general community. Ultimately individuals separated themselves from the mass, usually by remaining behind when the tide of humanity flowed back toward the border again. As we look farther east the migration becomes increasingly individualistic.

This is reflected in a recent complaint from South Chicago about an influx of *solos*, which means men unaccompanied by their families. They are quite unpopular among other Mexicans, largely because of the competition that they offer for women who have already been spoken for by the local Mexican males.

This industrial migration has its roots in the same general situation as that which has drawn agricultural workers north. Some jobs are either so unpleasant or so poorly paid (or both) that no one who has been long on the American scene will take them. European immigration largely ceased at the time of the first world war. Only two sources of cheap labor remained: Negroes and Mexicans. Both were enlisted in large numbers during and after the war. When the dark days of the twenties arrived nothing cold be done about the surplus Negro population other than to put it on relief. The Mexicans were more vulnerable, as many of them were not American citizens, and so could be deported. With the second world war the tide flowed northward again, and this time it appears to be here to stay. Most of the Mexicans in the North have become American citizens. As we will see, they are gradually getting their roots further and further into the life of Northern communities.

Chicago not only has the largest Mexican population of any Northern city, but what has happened there will be repeated on a smaller scale elsewhere.

The first Mexicans to come to Chicago were railroad track workers. A leader among them reports, "Only the old men who know nothing else and the young ones fresh from Mexico or the Southwest are now tamping ties."

The stockyards were a second field of employment. Here the avenues of advancement are said to be more open than in steel, but the proportion of Mexicans is declining.

The largest employers of Mexican labor in the Chicago areas have been the steel mills in South Chicago and Indiana Harbor. As "chippers" they did the hottest and dirtiest work. They also joined the unions, although they are not particularly active in union affairs, and have enjoyed the economic prosperity that has been the lot of steel workers in recent years. Many of their leaders do not feel that their advancement has been as rapid or has gone as far as it should. Their predecessors in the mills were the Poles, and the Poles have managed to hang on to the really good jobs. It is also said, by Mexicans, that they have not been as alert and as self-confident in their quest for promotion as they might have been. Apparently they are in steel to stay, at least for the foreseeable future.

The hotels are a relatively new field of work. In the past hotels have been designed and operated on the assumption that much cheap labor could be had. As other sources of willing workers at low pay dried up, Mexicans were employed in increasing numbers. They began as dishwashers, chambermaids, bus boys. Here, too, they have both joined the union and worked their way up. One page of the paper gotten out by the hotel workers' union is printed in Spanish. As for advancement, Mexicans are now working as waiters, headwaiters, chefs, stewards— and one of their number is chief steward of the Palmer House. In the meantime, hotel work is becoming less physically exhausting and much better remunerated.

From these basic occupations the Mexicans are gradually branching out into many lines of employment. According to a social worker in Chicago, more of the girls than the boys go to high school—and graduate into office work.

The increasing prosperity of the Mexicans in Chicago is reflected in the places where they don't live. Apparently they are departing from the deteriorated sections and are scattering out over the city into the neighborhoods where other people of similar incomes live. They move wherever they can get homes that they can afford to rent or buy.

In the North, Mexicans have always lived in porous rather than compact communities. That is, they do not bunch up solidly as the Italians have commonly done, or as the Jews and the Negroes have been compelled to do, but live intermingled with other nationalities.

The original Mexican colony in Chicago was around Halsted Street on the near West Side. However, in the long history of this section the Mexicans promise to be just one more in the procession of nationalities that have passed through. They were preceded by the Italians, and it looks as though they would be followed by the Negroes. Mexicans mingle in the neighborhood with Italians, Greeks, Lithuanians, and Negroes. Both the Methodist and Presbyterian churches for Mexicans are in this area.

Two social institutions have large Mexican contacts, although these are not intended exclusively for them. The South Chicago Community Center occupies what was originally the Bird Memorial Church. It is supported one-third by the Chicago Congregational Union and two-thirds by the Community Fund. Its strong points are its nursery school and its youth activities. An interesting feature is the "V" (for volunteer) Staff consisting of Mexican young people who share responsibility with the paid workers. Bright and lively are the adjectives that best describe both the building and the people in it.

Hull House has more dignity and suffers somewhat from its ancient architecture and the gloom of its surroundings, but appears to be as well worn as ever. The present head resident has had much of his social experience with Mexicans. The telephone operators and other helpers are Mexican.

At Hull House is the office of the Mexican American Council of Chicago. The preamble of its constitution reads:

We, the Mexican Americans of the Chicago area, are determined: To affirm faith in human rights and the dignity and worth of all men and women, and for these ends to practice justice and live in peace, and have resolved to organize our strength and hereby establish an organization to be called the Mexican American Council of Chicago. The purpose of the council is the better integration of the Mexican American in the life of the community, promotion of the welfare and aiding the development of all Mexican Americans in the Chicago area. The council shall be non-sectarian and non-partisan.

Just before my visit, the council had presented a program of Mexican music and dances in Thorne Hall of Northwestern University, with an accompanying talk on "Contributions of the Mexican People to Our American Heritage," by Dr. Louis Leal.

The Mexicans were first brought to Detroit in 1918 to work in the automobile factories. Their numbers climbed to 16,000 during the twenties and then dropped to half of that during the thirties. Detroit being a city of new industries, the employment opportunities have been varied. Most of the men came without their families, with the result that there has been more intermarriage with other groups than elsewhere.

There appear to be ties between the Mexicans of Detroit and those who "work in brass" in Port Huron and also with the settlements that have sprung up around the beet fields and orchards farther north.

Apparently some of the Mexicans in Detroit combine industry and agriculture; at least a considerable group were off picking cherries when we visited the city.

In Detroit we were given some insight into the problems of young people of Mexican ancestry, which are similar to those found in many other youth groups. If they go to college it is their decision and not that of their parents, and they are likely to go to a school where they already have a friend. They resent the crowding in many of their homes and also the inclination of many parents to tell them when they should come home. Often they meet the situation by moving out and living with someone else. This is not "running away from home," for the mother knows where the boy or girl is living, but a convenient way out of a situation that can be mutually embarrassing.

A steel mill brought 1,500 Mexicans to Lorain, Ohio, from Texas in 1923. This colony has been further recruited both from Texas and from the beet fields of Michigan. At first the people lived in the box cars in which they had arrived, but they have gradually moved up in the world without discarding many Mexican characteristics. According to Robert O. O'Brien, "American radios are covered with *serapes* and bits of Indian pottery. Stone hand mills grind our corn, which is cooked on gas and even electric stoves. American phonographs play South American tangos and Mexican marches. Mexican trunks (which are likely to be iron bound and forbidding) contain a mixture of objects, from new Sunday clothes to old country *sombreros*. Portable typewriters in vivid colors compete for space with bits of cactus from the Southwest. Bottles of medicine from Lorain doctors vie with patent medicines or Mexican 'teas' for position on the bathroom shelf. . . . American canned food is supplemented by *enchiladas, chile verde,* and *tamales.*"

The Spanish-speaking population of Lorain, which was formerly wholly Mexican, is now being enlarged by an influx of Puerto Ricans.

On a much smaller scale the same sort of thing is happening in Detroit and Chicago. An interested minister writes:

The Puerto Ricans, like the Mexicans, live largely in South Lorain. There is no strict segregation and both Mexicans and Puerto Ricans can be found throughout the city. The first 500 Puerto Rican men were brought to the city by the National Tube Company as contract labor in 1946. Since then their brothers and sisters, fathers and mothers and cousins by the dozens have followed them in a never-ending stream, until there are close to 4,000 here now. The majority work at "the Tube" or at Freuhauf, or on the railroads, but a number have found their way into other jobs. There are a number of Protestants among them and a few have found their way into established churches, chiefly the Presbyterian, which is the one most available. The language creates a problem, as only two Protestant ministers in the county speak Spanish, and neither are very fluent.

Here we see the beginning of a new cycle, but one quite similar to that through which the Mexicans are passing.

These Northern beachheads will probably go through a two-fold process of both growth and absorption. These *colonias* will multiply in number and increase in population simply because they will offer ambitious young Mexican Americans a chance to escape from the discriminations that they suffer along the border and to better themselves economically. Yet the more these isolated groups of Mexicans prosper the less Mexican will they become. In all likelihood it will be in the North and not on the border that Mexicans will be most completely made a part of the nation's life.

Rafael Palacios, former resident of Puerto Rico, now a New York free-lance artist specializing in book jackets and maps.

) CHAPTER 7 (

The Puerto Ricans Fly to New York

NEXT to Mexico, Puerto Rico offers the United States its most available source of cheap labor. Puerto Rico is a small island, three times the size of the state of Rhode Island, twice that of Long Island, somewhat smaller than the state of Connecticut. It is one of the most densely populated areas in the world, and from the economic angle is entitled to hang out a "standing room only" sign. New York is becoming the largest Puerto Rican city in the world, with a Puerto Rican population equal to 15 per cent of that of the island from which they came.

The Puerto Ricans are citizens of the United States, "with all the rights and privileges thereto pertaining." Some time ago I arrived in New York on a boat from Venezuela, thinking myself the only United States citizen on the passenger list. The immigration inspector looked at me and announced, "I will take the citizen first," at which a Puerto Rican stepped up and presented his papers. United States citizenship does for the Puerto Ricans something similar to what Roman citizenship did for the Apostle Paul. It is a great help in getting around.

The Puerto Ricans come far, but fast. The island's nearest point in continental United States is Key West, which is a bit farther from San Juan than Chicago is from New York. The trip to New York is 1,500 miles, which is approximately the distance from New York to Omaha. Today the quickest and cheapest way to make the trip is by air. Since the war the fare has been as low as $75 on the regular lines and $35 on non-scheduled flights. Instead of going through Ellis Island, the Puerto Ricans land at Idlewild Airport. This is the world's first large scale movement of population by air.

For this recent spurt in immigration there are three reasons. Puerto Rico is overcrowded. By exporting workers she increases the available jobs and food for those who remain. The mainland is suffering from a labor shortage, especially in employment where the work is muscle-taxing and the pay low. The development of mass air travel has made the trip fast and painless. Sometimes only five hours elapse between departure from San Juan and arrival in New York.

The vast majority of the migrants had jobs in Puerto Rico, and fairly good jobs judged by local standards. According to a careful investigation the first job in New York averages double the wage of the last job in Puerto Rico, with a jump from $20 a week on the island to $40 a week in the United States not at all unusual.[1]

The lure of New York, where over 80 per cent of the Puerto Ricans settle, is more than a matter of dollars. Pretty pictures put out by the airlines do not attract them so much as the letters of friends and relatives and the stories told by Puerto Ricans who have come home to

[1] Most of the data in this chapter is from *The Puerto Rican Journey*, by C. Wright Mills, Clarence Senior, and Rose Kohn Goldsen. New York, Harper and Brothers, 1950.

visit—and to brag about their new estate. Even though they may share in it in only a slight way, the life and movement of New York appeal to them—the picture shows, the beaches, even the subway. Compared to Manhattan Island, San Juan, one of the brightest of Latin American cities, is a drab place.

On a hot summer's night I discovered six rides ranging from a merry-go-round to a Ferris wheel and an aerial torpedo, which appeared to turn one upside down only really didn't, going full blast on a vacant lot in the Puerto Rican section of the Bronx. Everything was running at capacity, and everybody seemed to be having a wonderful time. It was reminiscent of the early years of this century, when Americans hung on open streetcars like iron-filings on a magnet to get to amusement parks where they could be swished through the air in strange ways. Most of the people "doing the rides" that night in the Bronx probably had not yet achieved automobiles.

Curiously, few Puerto Ricans appear to be disillusioned by New York. They have heard about snow storms and six-story walk-ups on the island. They are accustomed to living close to other people, and rather like crowds. As for noise, they delight in it. Despite the problems that confront them, the Puerto Ricans of New York strongly prefer where they are to where they were.

Most of the immigrants are in the middle years of life, ranging from young people ready to look for their first jobs to parents with a couple of children. Both old people and teen-agers are scarce. The venturesome years are the migrating years. Most of the families come from the cities of San Juan and Ponce, few from the country. They are already city-wise. Both their education and their pay is above that of the island as a whole. Their background is industrial rather than rural, which may explain why they are not disappointed with life in New York.

Although the two sexes are numerically equal in Puerto Rico, over a third more women than men have come to New York. In addition to the normal number of housewives, there have been many whose marriages have been ended by death, divorce, or desertion. In Spanish lands, the unattached mature woman has had a difficult role. If she lived with her family she was likely to be dominated by it; if she lived by herself she was regarded with disapproval. For these women New York has meant a larger degree of personal freedom to earn their own living and make their own way. New York is a city of refuge for those who have been overdominated by their families. There women of all nationalities are free to be themselves with the minimum of attention from onlookers, who are busy with their own affairs.

Ever since the United States took over Puerto Rico in 1898 her people have been coming to this country. Puerto Ricans have been a part of New York, and New York has figured prominently in the life of the island for a good many years. The new factor is the volume of this migration; what was once a trickle is now a fast flowing stream. Few came during the war, but in 1945, 13,000 more people traveled from the island to the mainland than journeyed in the opposite direction. The next year this figure jumped to 39,000, then dropped slightly, but for 1951 it was 49,000. In New York city there are somewhere between 300,000 and 350,000 Puerto Ricans and the children of Puerto Ricans. There is no apparent slackening in this flow of humanity.

Why do 80 per cent of the Puerto Ricans remain in New York city? Probably for much the same reasons that many of their predecessors, particularly the Irish, the Jews, the Italians, have lingered for some years in the metropolis before venturing into the hinterland. All immigrants have heard about New York city as a place where there is lots of money and people can get rich quick. In New York they have friends and relatives who speak their language and who will look after them.

New York is accustomed to people who speak strange tongues and eat strange foods. It is, from necessity, a tolerant town. Actually in New York the minorities are in a majority. It also offers a larger market for unskilled and semiskilled labor than any other American city. Except for clothing, New York is not a manufacturing center. It requires relatively few skilled craftsmen. It does not create, but rather distributes. It is also a place where millions come for personal services. What New York needs is a lot of people who are willing to perform relatively simple operations. For centuries this has been the lot of the last to arrive, who at present are the Puerto Ricans.

From necessity, most immigrants begin on the bottom rung of the ladder. As far as their status and the significance of their jobs are concerned, most Puerto Ricans step down rather than up when they come to New York. This is due primarily to difficulty with the language and to the lack of the skills that are highly rewarded in this country. As we have seen, the new job pays better in dollars than the old one but is likely to detract from rather than add to one's self respect. New York offers money in the pocket rather than nourishment for one's ego. And there is evidence that many of the Puerto Rican immigrants do not rise far above the place where they start in this country, although their children do.

The first group of Puerto Ricans to come to New York were stevedores who worked on the Brooklyn docks and lived nearby. More recently the starting occupations have been in restaurants and hotels for men, in the garment trades for women. A Roman Catholic priest oversimplified the matter when he said, "The men wash dishes; the women sew," but this is a vivid way of describing what happens to many of the newcomers.

The Puerto Ricans have no particular aptitude for restaurant and hotel work but have entered these fields because the jobs were there.

They have not done at all badly. The Waldorf-Astoria employs 300 Puerto Ricans, which is 12 per cent of its labor force. The men work as bus boys, waiters, coffee and salad men, ice cream makers, pastry cooks, and chefs, and the women as chambermaids. The personnel manager rates them as equal to the other employees in cleanliness, productivity, and punctuality.

Many Puerto Rican men and some women are found in assembly work and in processing. One establishment in the Bronx employs 400 Puerto Ricans as punch pressers, cutters, spot welders, and on assembly lines and in packaging. Several of the foremen are Puerto Ricans.

Puerto Rican women have always distinguished themselves in needle-work. They bring with them to New York sharp eyes and nimble fingers. Signs such as this are common, *"Operadoras con experiencia en blusas. Trabajo por sección,"* which means that piecework is available for women with experience on blouses. Contrary to the sweatshop traditions of the past, the garment industry in New York has excellent employment conditions, while the two unions, the International Ladies' Garment Workers and the Amalgamated Clothing Workers, are famous for their cooperation with the employers to improve conditions in the industry and for the educational and social programs that they offer their members.

The Puerto Ricans do not come to this country to undercut those who are already here. Although they are not "joiners" by tradition, they go into labor unions quickly and apparently unanimously. The unions in the hotel and garment industry have Spanish-speaking locals and print part of their papers in Spanish.

Although the mass of the Puerto Ricans have humble employment, individuals have gone far. Puerto Rican stenographers are both common and popular in New York. In Spanish-speaking neighborhoods the smaller stores are commonly Puerto Rican owned. The children of the early comers are doing well in the professions and in business. Given time, it is reasonable to expect that the Puerto Ricans will prosper as have other immigrant groups before them.

As the last comers, the Puerto Ricans have been compelled to take such living accommodations as they could get. From the point of view of housing they have arrived at a peculiarly inopportune time, when even those with financial resources and powerful connections have had a hard time finding a place to live. On top of this, the Puerto Ricans have frequently found themselves right in the path of large-scale building and housing developments. Their original place of residence in Brooklyn simply isn't there any more!

To find living quarters that no one else wanted for a rent that they could afford to pay has been most difficult. The more recently arrived Puerto Ricans live under the worst conditions to be found in New York city. The first step is to move in with somebody else, usually a relative newcomer. The "port of entry" for many if not most Puerto Ricans is East Harlem. Here the prevailing type of building is the six-story walk-up cold water flat.

The Jews, the Italians, the Russians, the Negroes have come and also largely gone. The procession of many feet has worn the steps, multitudinous voices in assorted tongues have echoed in the hallways, families have come from many quarters of the globe and then moved on to better things, but the old foundations and the ancient walls still stand to welcome yet another influx from afar.

However, it is possible to exaggerate tenement conditions. We have passed through dingy hallways to tidy rooms, and we have heard of irate housewives vainly pursuing cockroaches over immaculate floors. It should be said that Puerto Ricans are accustomed to living in close quarters and that the per square foot population may not be any greater in Harlem than in San Juan. A large factor of difference is the sun. On the island it purifies and cleanses. The garbage that the birds of the air do not take care of is sterilized by natural heat. In New York the sun is less powerful and has less chance to neutralize filth. The cold weather is also a new experience and one in which ancient housing does not help.

Like the Mexicans, and for the same reasons, the Puerto Ricans live in mixed neighborhoods. Rarely do they constitute more than 50 per cent of the population of a given area, and the longer they are here and the better their incomes the more they mingle with the general population. In East Harlem they have Italians and Negroes for neighbors.

The first step up from East Harlem is likely to be the southeast section of the Bronx. Here the housing is better, the streets wider, and the sun more effective. The neighbors are Jews and Negroes. From here the Puerto Ricans scatter out to lower Manhattan, to Brooklyn, to the West Side, to Washington Heights, almost anywhere. Two-thirds of the public schools of the city have some Puerto Rican children. The long term prospect points toward a general diffusion of the Puerto Ricans among the population.

In this process there is one catch. The Puerto Rican whose complexion is light can rent or buy almost anywhere that he can afford to live. His problem is almost wholly economic. But the Puerto Rican who is of darker complexion does not fare so well. For him East Harlem and the Bronx are likely to be more permanent places of residence. Curiously, there is just one way that he can escape from being classified as a Negro, and that is to retain his Spanish speech and to pose as a newcomer from overseas. New York extends rather better treatment to the foreign Negro than to the American Negro. If one's face is dark, there is profit in professing the Moslem faith and aspiring to being taken as a Moor!

New York can frighten anyone. We once employed a most self-confident girl from Minneapolis who insisted on being thoroughly briefed on where she was going before she would venture onto the sidewalks of New York. The newly arrived Puerto Rican is likely to be overwhelmed by the sights and sounds around him. The only people with whom he feels safe are his fellow countrymen. New York assumes that everybody can read English. Ten-car subway trains are manned by a crew of three. If one can neither read nor speak English, he is in a bad way, and is not likely to venture far alone. Puerto Rican women sometimes walk for a mile or two to get to a hospital or some other destination simply because they feel far more sure of themselves on foot than in a subway or on a bus.

During the first years, the life of a Puerto Rican family moves in a small circle. Most social contacts are "on the block." Groceries are purchased near at hand, preferably from small stores in which Spanish is spoken. Rice, beans, and plantains are the chief items of diet and the frying pan the chief kitchen utensil. If there are neighbors in New York who have also been neighbors in Puerto Rico, that is a comforting circumstance and gives one a sense of security. The first job is likely to be where fellow Puerto Ricans are employed and where the boss speaks Spanish. What looks to be a plunge into the alien life of New York turns out to be a dip into a Puerto Rican pool in a secluded corner of the metropolis. But so has it ever been with immigrants.

Adjustments come gradually, with the younger members of the family leading. The children are very shy at first, but gradually become as fresh as the other urchins of New York. Ultimately even the women achieve a sense of freedom. A Puerto Rican student reports that they "hop around much more freely at parties" in New York than back home.

Competent social observers believe Puerto Ricans will make an exceptionally quick adjustment to American life. Favoring circumstances

are their United States citizenship and their disposition to scatter out into the American community as soon as they master the language and acquire the financial resources for such a move.

The concentration of the Puerto Rican population in New York city is probably temporary. It can be argued that New York is not America and that no group can become integrated into the national life until it gets away from the banks of the Hudson. Already 20 per cent of the Puerto Rican migrants are going elsewhere, and in a way that is both interesting and significant. The Government of Puerto Rico is undertaking to direct the migration of its people and to aid them in adjusting to life on the mainland. This is something new under the sun. It is an endeavor to relieve the overcrowding on the island by discovering employment opportunities for Puerto Ricans in all the states of the union.

During the war years Bahamians and Jamaicans were brought into this country under contract for the harvesting of crops, particularly sugar beets and various fruits. Although they were available, Puerto Ricans were not used in this way. The reason was given by the president of a Florida growers' association: "The vast difference between Bahama Island labor and the domestic, including the Puerto Rican, is that (it) . . . can be diverted and sent home if it does not work." In other words, Puerto Ricans could not be deported at the end of the season. Since the war, however, Puerto Ricans have been brought to the mainland under contract in increasing numbers.

The Report of the President's Commission on Migratory Labor states:

Beginning in a small scale in 1946 and 1947, Puerto Ricans have been drawn increasingly into the domestic seasonal labor force, reaching a peak in 1950, the last year covered by the report, of 8,500 or more. Before 1950 the Puerto Rican contract workers were located mainly in the Northeast; in the year 1950 some 5,300 were contracted for sugar beet work in Michigan. Technically, the movement of Puerto Ricans, either seasonal or permanent, does not require negotiation of work contracts or prior certification of labor shortage. Nevertheless, in its desire to protect its citizens as much as possible, the Puerto Rican Government has insisted on both work contracts and certification of labor need before approving recruitment of its people.

As contract laborers, the Puerto Ricans enjoy both the rights that have been secured for Mexicans, Bahamians, and others, and the rights that are theirs as American citizens. They are guaranteed 150 hours of work for each four week period covered by the contract at the prevailing rate, but with an agreed upon minimum that must be paid, and are protected as to travel, housing, and discrimination. Until quite recently, no American migrants have had such assurances as this. But, also, as an American citizen the Puerto Rican cannot be deported. If he chooses to remain in the community after his contract period is up, that is his privilege. And that is exactly what happens. As the Mexicans are establishing beachhead settlements where they first came as migrants, so are the Puerto Ricans. In the preceding chapter, we noted how this is happening in Lorain, Ohio.

The circumstances for this air-borne agricultural migration are most fortunate in that the slack season on sugar cane cultivation in Puerto Rico comes at the same time as the busy season in sugar beets on the mainland, so that the same people can cultivate cane sugar in Puerto Rico and beet sugar in Michigan. Quick transport makes possible an economical use of labor in both places.

The Government of Puerto Rico is also looking for permanent employment for its people in the states. It has gotten out a most attractive brochure announcing, "Capable hands can be flown to your plant from Puerto Rico, U.S.A." This states, "In Bridgeport, Connecticut, there are around 3,000 Puerto Rican industrial workers. In Philadelphia and Camden, around 4,000. Close to 1,500 men and women from Puerto Rico work in Cleveland, between 6,000 and 7,000 in Chicago. Between 400 and 500 of Milwaukee's foundry workers are from Puerto Rico, U.S.A." This publication also contains pictures of Puerto Ricans happily at work and testimonials from satisfied employers. Wabash Frozen Foods in Chicago reports that they are "superior in punctuality, cleanliness, and productivity to previous workers on the same jobs." The superintendent of employment at National Tube, Lorain, Ohio, is most enthusiastic: "They're tops. Many of them served in the U.S. fighting forces during the recent war. Most have had at least a grade school education. Many have high school certificates, and the University of Puerto Rico is pretty well represented." The only drawback to Puerto

Rican labor is that rather more time is needed to break them in than is true of groups that have become adjusted to industrial work. The Art Steel Company "rates Puerto Ricans equal in productivity and punctuality to others, although some of them take slightly longer in learning machine operations, due to deficient English."

Until quite recently there have been few industries in Puerto Rico, with the result that few Puerto Ricans have had the type of training in machine work that is needed on the mainland. Puerto Rico is endeavoring to remedy this situation by developing eleven vocational schools that will take care of 6,000 students. One school alone has an enrollment of 3,000 students at the present time and offers training in 21 basic fields.

In the meantime, the problem is to direct unskilled and semi-skilled workers to the places where they are most needed. To this end the Government of Puerto Rico maintains labor offices in New York, Chicago, and Los Angeles. The New York Office is a large and busy place, serving three functions. It issues certificates of citizenship to Puerto Ricans who are entitled to them, which is a great aid in securing employment. Puerto Ricans who desire work are interviewed in Spanish and then referred, along with the appropriate information, to the state and federal employment services, which have few Spanish-speaking workers, or directly to employers. Any Puerto Rican who has a problem is interviewed in Spanish and then referred to the New York social agency best equipped to handle it.

As an exhibition of human thoughtfulness, this office compels admiration. As American citizens, Puerto Ricans are entitled to go to the state and national employment service and to social agencies, but as strangers in New York speaking little if any English, they are not likely to do so. They feel free to talk in Spanish with the representatives of their own government, and these in turn direct them to the right places. Anyone acquainted with the complexities of the social agencies of a great city will appreciate what this means.

But the Puerto Rican Government is going even further; it is seeking to interpret its people to their fellow citizens of the mainland. It has published a most attractive picture booklet of 64 pages entitled "Know Your Fellow American Citizen from Puerto Rico." The foreword states, "This booklet has been prepared as an aid to understanding the background of the relatively small migration of Puerto Ricans to the U. S. mainland. As American citizens most of them have come to the States in search of jobs, schooling, or commercial opportunities. As American citizens they must struggle for a livelihood and for acceptance in much the same way that their mainland neighbors do. It is hoped that this booklet will be helpful to neighbors, social workers, writers, teachers, clergymen, and men of good will who are helping these newcomers adjust properly to the opportunities and expectations of their adopted communities."[2]

Obviously this industrial migration is relatively new, which means that jobs may not have been thoroughly mastered and in many instances the families have not been sent for. The major significance of this movement lies in the future. Puerto Ricans will be used increasingly to meet the labor shortages that may develop in our industrial centers. They will be better and better prepared for their tasks and will ultimately work as individuals instead of as groups as at present. It is quite likely that in a few years the Puerto Ricans will be as well integrated into the total life of the nation as their predecessors are now—the Irish, the Germans, and the Scandinavians.

When several hundred thousand people migrate from an island to a continent, changing their mode of livelihood and modifying their

[2] This may be obtained without charge by writing to the Office of the Government of Puerto Rico, 1026 Seventeenth St., N. W., Washington, D. C.

way of life, their religious life will not go unaffected. Other groups have met this situation in one of two ways. The Irish, the Germans, the Poles have been even more loyal to their ancestral faith in the new home than in the old. They have brought the church with them. The Chinese, Japanese, Mexicans, and, to a large extent, the Jews, have left their church behind them. The small proportion of Puerto Ricans who are Protestants have brought their church and their ministers with them, while the 85 per cent who are nominally Roman Catholic have for the most part left their church behind them. Unlike many other immigrant groups, Puerto Rican Catholics have established no parishes of their own in this country.

The Roman Catholic Church enjoyed a religious monopoly in Puerto Rico for four centuries. It was then disestablished without being persecuted. Instead of facing persecution it was called on to meet competition, which crept up on it in an unspectacular way.

The attitude of the Puerto Ricans toward the Roman Catholic Church has two sides. Outwardly they conform. They use the church for baptisms, weddings (when they can afford it), and funerals. They enjoy church festivals. The church is a place where they see their friends and are seen by their neighbors. Underneath, however, there is much resentment toward the church. They use it but do not love it. They feel that the church is in some ways alien to themselves and that it has imposed upon them.

A Roman Catholic priest gave me a clue as to why this might be so. He said, "The Germans are loyal to the church as an institution, but the Irish and the Latins give their loyalty more to the priest as a person." Organizations as such mean little; personal ties are all powerful.

We have found no explanation of why the Roman Catholic Church cannot recruit priests in a land where the population has outrun the employment possibilities. For some reason, the clerical life does not appeal to Puerto Rican boys. The Roman Catholic Church cannot export priests from the island to the United States simply because it has none to spare.

The reverse situation prevails among Puerto Rican Protestants. Although the most that they can claim is a membership of 200,000 in a population of 2,200,000, they do not lack for native leadership. Even the theological seminary that trains ministers for the major denominations now has a Puerto Rican president with the Puerto Ricans a majority on its faculty. Only a handful of North Americans serve the mission boards on the island; from the point of view of the common man, Protestantism is more indigenous and much closer to the people than is the foreign-dominated Roman Catholic Church. As a consequence, it is natural for Puerto Rican young men to enter the ministry—and enough of them do so to take care of the Protestant churches on the island and also to minister to the Puerto Rican congregations on the mainland. It is heartening to see how splendidly the close relationship between the Protestant clergy and the laity is paying off at this point.

Puerto Rican Protestantism has the further virtue of practical ecumenicity. The various denominational mission boards arrived on the island simultaneously at the time of the American occupation. Instead of competing with one another, the major groups divided the island between them on a geographical basis. They have trained their ministers together and published a common paper. For years it has been assumed that when a Protestant moved from *el campo Metodista* (the country of the Methodists) to *el campo Presbyteriano* (the country of the Presbyterians) he would shift his denominational affiliations accordingly. This type of loyalty has proved invaluable in the present migration. Instead of hunting for their own brand of Protestantism, the Puerto Ricans have been ready to accept what was offered them, asking only that it be Protestant.

Turning our attention to the mainland, according to the best estimates available, based on research sponsored by Columbia University, the Puerto Rican population of New York city is 83 per cent nominally Roman Catholic, 9 per cent Protestant, 5 per cent adherents of Pentecostal sects that are graphically described by the Puerto Ricans as *los aleluyas,* and 2 per cent spiritualist. These figures are on the basis of adherents rather than active or actual members. The New York City Missionary Society has been able to discover 62 Puerto Rican Protestant churches that reported a membership of 7,856 in 1949, with a slightly smaller number enrolled in Sunday school. The number of churches, membership, and Sunday school enrollment have increased steadily since then. The multiplicity of Protestant congregations has in it elements of both strength and weakness, as we will see.

Protestantism in Puerto Rican New York is kaleidoscopic in its range and color—as we have seen demonstrated on successive Sundays.

On an August Sunday afternoon we visited La Iglesia Cristiana del Valle (The Christian Church in the Valley) in the Bronx. At first we thought that we would have either to stand up or sit in a front pew, which might be embarrassing, but a thoughtful soul pointed to a folding chair, which we placed in the aisle, inwardly hoping that the Fire Department would not look in that afternoon. Some 150 people had been in session for at least half an hour before we arrived, and probably continued long after the forty-five minutes that we spent with them. The range of age was from three on up. When we came in a woman was singing a solo, with the help of a loud-speaker. While we were there, she and two men "presided" in succession. The meeting was a mingling of songs, some without either announcement or books; prayer, more or less in concert; and sheer ecstasy. At times the congregation clapped their hands with a powerful rhythm. As the meeting progressed, several women left their seats to move down the aisle with a revolving step that was a sort of slow whirl. There was no discoverable intellectual content to the service. The people were expressing their emotions even more freely than they might have done at the nearby Yankee Stadium. For many of them it must have been the high spot of the week. Here drab lives were rising above themselves through the emotional escape of religious ecstasy. In this the Puerto Ricans are not alone; similar services can be found among other groups.

Of a similar but much milder nature were the three street meetings within half a mile of one another that we discovered at dusk on a Sunday night, and the services of two small groups that were huddled together in earnest prayer in garage-sized rooms on the same night. At least here Puerto Ricans were responding to one type of Puerto Rican leadership.

In striking contrast to this was the Sunday morning service that we attended in the same neighborhood at La Luterana Iglesia España (The Spanish Lutheran Church). Here was both order and reverence. The service began with the singing of the tune "Ein Feste Burg" in full-throated Spanish and proceeded heartily in accordance with a Spanish version of the prayer book of the United Lutheran Church. But the formality was well tinctured with friendliness. After the sermon the minister spoke more casually, calling on another minister in the congregation to say a few words, which were followed by some remarks from a layman. The congregation appeared both friendly and prosperous.

About a score of Protestant churches minister to the Puerto Ricans of New York. Among these are the four Spanish churches sponsored by the New York City Mission Society, an interdenominational organization that has also given general leadership through careful study of the

Spanish-speaking population and the effort to meet new needs. Two common procedures with foreign language groups have not worked at all well with the Puerto Ricans. One is for the foreign-speaking group to use an English-speaking church for Sunday afternoon or other meetings. The social gap between the newly arrived Puerto Ricans and the old established congregations has made this difficult. We discovered a Puerto Rican congregation meeting in the building of a Lutheran Church of German antecedents on East 119th Street on Sunday afternoon, but without benefit of a sign! Another procedure has been for the incoming population to take over the churches or synagogues of the departing population. Unfortunately, the Puerto Ricans have settled in two areas of New York that are almost totally devoid of religious structures of any sort. Their immediate predecessors have been Jews, and apparently rather irreligious Jews. To find meeting places for Protestant congregations both in East Harlem and in the southeast Bronx has been most difficult, while to clear away existing structures and build a church in New York is terribly expensive. The result has been to give Protestantism a rather lower degree of visibility in the Puerto Rican neighborhoods than it really deserves.

As the Puerto Ricans scatter out, they face the choice of either returning to distinctly Puerto Rican churches or of affiliating themselves with local English-speaking congregations. No marked trend in either direction has as yet developed. So far as the city itself is concerned, well dressed Puerto Ricans who speak English would be welcome in practically any church.

The East Harlem Protestant Parish was born of the conviction on the part of some students in Union Theological Seminary that Protestantism should do something for East Harlem, in many ways the most neglected section of the city. These students have lived among the people. Accepting the "live-in-the-block" custom, they have started three store

front churches whose general crudity matches that of the general surroundings. They found both the Negroes and the Puerto Ricans of East
Harlem eager to find someone who would listen to their woes. They
also found that much could be done to help these people, particularly
by standing up for them and with them as against landlords, city officials, and the police. The last named have often been careless and even
brutal in their dealings with the boys of the neighborhood. Now when
the police round up a group they ask them where they go to church,
and if they reply "East Harlem Protestant Parish" they are quite likely
to let them go!

Probably the greatest lesson of the East Harlem Parish is that these
people are more or less lost in a new world and that their supreme need
is for a sense of personal security. They will support a church that sup-
ports them. And here is a place where the church has much to do on
every level—from inspiring a cleanup campaign to agitating against the
use of narcotics, from tending babies to conducting meaningful
worship.

Presbyterian Labor Temple, in a crowded downtown section of New
York, carries on a varied ministry among all nationalities and faiths that
its leaders call "symphony in a democracy." A Puerto Rican minister,
the Reverend Salvador Bernart, is assigned to this staff to help Puerto
Ricans in the neighborhood in their orientation to living in New York.
This is done through job counsel, lessons in English, and invitations to
participate in the fellowship. The Governor of Puerto Rico, the Hon-
orable Luis Muñoz Marin, has written to Labor Temple in appreciation
of their help.

The Puerto Ricans appear to be more susceptible to the appeal of
Protestantism in New York than in San Juan. They are groping for
something that Protestantism possesses—a sense of both religious and
social security.

Protestantism when it is true to itself is always evangelical. It proclaims a God who is concerned about men, and who will enter intimately into their lives if given the chance. The Roman Catholic God is awe-inspiring but remote. The Protestant God need not lack grandeur and is never far away. The genius of Protestantism is the closeness of the ties between God and man.

Even more effective than its religious teaching is the social aspect of Protestantism. The church is something to which you definitely belong. It is not a vague conception; it is a company of people who care for one another. Here the individual is always important. Whatever his workaday lot, in the church he has status in the eyes of both God and man. Here is a basis for emotional security, a rock to which one may anchor. The bewildering immensity of a city such as New York and the individual helplessness of those who have come to it from another land accentuate the need for religious fellowship. And this is what gives power to many little groups whose expression of religion may seem most bizarre.

The principles that we have been trying to state are well illustrated in the true story of Gustavo and Carmen, to whom we will give the fictitious name of Blanco. The fact that they are Cubans rather than Puerto Ricans rather improves the drama.

Gustavo worked for the railroad as a ticket-seller and minor accountant. He was a nominal Roman Catholic. Carmen's father had broken with the church, and had advised his children to seek their own religion. Carmen had a sister who was married and living in Yonkers. When Gustavo had some time off, they came to the States for a visit. Being pregnant, Carmen consulted a doctor, who urged her not to risk the trip back to Havana, but to have her child here. As Carmen was not averse to giving birth to an American citizen, this was done.

Returning to Cuba, they found that the declining business of the railroad did not offer much of a future for Gustavo, and so they decided to take advantage of the baby's citizenship and return to New York, perhaps permanently. They flew to Miami and then took a bus to New York, "so we could see the country," Carmen explained.

Looking for work was not too happy an experience for Gustavo. His English is not fluent, and he is temperamentally shy. Instead of working with figures and books he has had to adjust himself to operating a machine. He began at $37.50 a week but has now worked up to $42 a week, a good wage in Cuba but not in New York. He and Carmen have a three room apartment on upper Columbus Avenue "with the bathtub in the kitchen," and the rent is $38 a month.

"I love the United States—but *this* is not the United States!" Carmen frequently exclaims. "We must get out into the country, the real country!" But that is not easy. Her immediate problem is to improve Gustavo's English—her own is rather good. Fortunately he is employed where there are no other Spanish-speaking workers, and so must use English. He tried night school but felt that it was not giving him what he needed. At present Carmen is working with him diligently every night. The baby is now two, and before long may take a hand with his father's education.

Carmen has been afraid of her neighbors and somewhat afraid of New York. She dreads the idea of her boy growing up "on the street." In her insecurity she has turned toward religion. She went to Mass. The Roman Catholic Church seemed far away and remote from her problems. She sampled *los aleluyas,* but her intelligence rebelled. Then she stumbled upon the Lutherans. Carmen realized that at last she had found the faith that could answer her needs. She says, "They have the same atmosphere of reverence as the Catholic Church, but they know what they believe—and they are friendly."

Here was what Carmen and Gustavo needed—faith and fellowship.

Carmen studied the catechism and was confirmed, and Gustavo followed her example. Last summer she helped with a Vacation Bible School, and when the minister went on his vacation the Blancos moved into the parsonage to look after things until he returned. What has happened to Gustavo and Carmen happens to thousands of others like them. They have deep needs to which only Protestantism has a satisfactory answer.

But Puerto Ricans have much to give as well as to receive. This is shown in the story of Elba Arias, now Mrs. Paul Benson. She grew up in the Presbyterian church in Lares, Puerto Rico, and attended the Polytechnic Institute at San Germán, a school that was established by the Presbyterians and that still, even though it has become a private enterprise, has a majority of Presbyterian trustees. For two years she worked on the Presbyterian rural life project at El Guacio, where she met a worker from the states, Paul Benson, who was a Lutheran of missionary parentage. After completing her term at El Guacio, she followed her family to Lorain, Ohio, where her father owns a grocery store and her brother-in-law has a restaurant. She found employment as a nurses' aide at St. Mary's Hospital. She and Paul were married in the summer of 1951. While he was completing his course at the Augustana Theological Seminary in Rock Island, Illinois, she took another year of college. In June, 1952, they left for South America, where they will be permanently stationed in either Uruguay or Chile as missionaries representing a combined venture on the part of several Lutheran bodies. Thus the evangelical seed that was planted in Puerto Rico and nourished in Lorain, Ohio, will bear abundant fruit in South America.

Youthful leaders in training with the Division of Home Missions, NCCC, before beginning their work among migrants.

) CHAPTER 8 (

The Lesser Streams

So FAR we have considered three groups of Spanish-speaking Americans: those whose ancestors had already established themselves in the West before it passed under the sovereignty of the United States; those who have crossed over from Mexico; and those who have flown over from Puerto Rico, arriving with the full rights of citizenship. We will now meet a fourth group, those who have come here from the other countries of Latin America. Although their numbers are relatively few, they exert a considerable influence on our relations to the countries to the south of us.

The most numerous of these are the Cubans. During the latter part of the nineteenth century the making of "Havana" cigars moved over from Cuba to Florida. A large colony of men whose deft fingers rolled the then popular cigar established themselves first at Key West and later at Tampa. The advent of cigar making machinery and the rise of the cigarette have reduced the number employed in this skilled trade to relatively small numbers, but the children of the original cigar makers have entered other occupations and have prospered generally. Today Tampa is the most cosmopolitan and industrialized city of Florida. Approximately one-third of its people speak Spanish.

The Cubans have followed a pattern of settlement quite different from that of the Mexicans and Puerto Ricans. In the portion of Tampa known as Ybor City they have established a distinctly Latin cultural center of their own, which has been reinforced by immigration direct from Spain and from Italy. The dominant social influences are the Cuban and Spanish clubs, which have ornate buildings and which provide many services for their members, including medical care for a monthly fee. Children do not ordinarily learn English until they enter the public schools. Girls are carefully chaperoned. Restaurants serving Spanish and Italian food attract the winter tourist. Here is a bit of authentic Latin atmosphere in the midst of America.

Only 10 per cent of the people of Ybor City attend the Roman Catholic Church. The attitudes of the rest range from indifference to positive antagonism, with the latter predominant. Many have broken with the church completely and even bury their dead without benefit of priest, minister, or prayer.

Various approaches have been made to the 50,000 Cubans, Spaniards, and Italians of the Tampa area by various groups, including the Methodists and the Evangelical United Brethren. A most successful venture has been the Ybor City Presbyterian Mission, where the Reverend Walter B. Passiglia has labored since 1935. Here is a trilingual church with a trilingual pastor. The largest service of the week is on Sunday morning and in English, but there is also a Spanish service on Wednesday night and one in Italian on Thursday night. The pastor, a Sicilian, as are most Italians in Tampa, is a graduate of Union Theological Seminary, Richmond, Virginia, a Southern Presbyterian school.

The greatest evidence of the success of this mission is its achievements in the area where the Roman Catholic Church has been pitiably weak in its work with Spanish-speaking people—the recruiting of the ministry. It has sent three of its boys and their well trained wives into the ministry, and two of its girls into Christian vocations. Its faith is catching; its concept of the ministry as a life of service is alluring.

Around New York city are a considerable number of Cubans and also of people from the Dominican Republic and the Central and South American republics, but they appear to have no group consciousness nor organizations. The Cubans and Dominicans in particular have been lost in the flood of Puerto Ricans who have swept into the city, and follow the same pattern of moving up the economic ladder and out from the more congested areas as soon as they can afford it.

The students who are coming to our colleges and universities from Latin America number approximately 10,000. They may be most significant from the point of view of international relations.

The role of the student in Latin America is far different from that of students in this country. Here nobody takes the political views of students very seriously. Their vote is not large enough to excite our politicians. In the republics to the south of us, student attitudes often decide the fate of a government. I traveled in South America with a passport in which I was described as a "student." The British laughed at this designation, but the South American officials took it seriously and treated me with more courtesy than would be the lot of a Spanish-speaking student in this country. However, when I came to a country where the students had unsuccessfully tried to throw the dictator out, I registered in the hotel as a "professor," but the management had trouble with my writing and told the police I was a *petrolero*, or oil man, the safest occupation for an American in that country.

There are several reasons for the political importance of students in

Latin America. They are a small and rather intimate group. Their parents are the people of power. The result is that the students feel a sense of responsibility for their country such as no group could know in the United States. When they start to this country to attend school, they leave home as important people. They are accustomed to being taken seriously. Too often that illusion perishes when they reach our shores. In Colombia I traveled for some days with a well dressed and charming student who was endeavoring to master English against his arrival in the United States. I have always wondered what happened to him when he landed in New Orleans. His face was quite dark.

We are likely to misunderstand the motives and attitudes of these students. For one thing, Latin America has nothing in the nature of the American liberal arts college. There are numerous *colegios*, many run by our mission boards, but in Spanish *colegio* does not mean "college" in our sense, but just "school." The Latin American student gets his *bachillerato* at the end of what we would call high school, and then proceeds immediately to the professional school of the university. Higher education is not thought of in terms of personal development but as a means for entering a profession that will give one both social prestige and a means of earning a good living. Possibly they are simply more frank about their aims than students in this country.

This attitude is reinforced by the expectations with which students look toward this country. They rate us tops in everything mechanical. They love our automobiles, our electric refrigerators, and all our gadgets. They admire our engineers and are convinced that our dentists are the best in the world. Unfortunately, they see this side of American life in such a clear light that our other characteristics are lost in the shadows. Before leaving home they have been indoctrinated with the stereotype that North Americans are by nature uncultured, unmannerly, unphilosophical, and utterly materialistic. They welcome our machinery, but they discount our ideals. On the basis of the movies that they have seen and the Americans whom they have met, this is not as unfair a generalization as it might seem.

What happens to these students after they reach our shores may be important to future relations between their country and ours.

In Buenos Aires I called upon Dr. Alfredo Palacios, who was at that time the fountainhead of anti-Americanism in Latin America. I found a proud man who had much prestige, particularly with the students of the South American countries. I learned that he had once visited New York for a few days. The one friend whom he had in this country could not be found. Dr. Palacios spoke no English, and had a horrible time. One can imagine his experience with taxi drivers, subway employees, police, and waiters. He has hated our country ever since.

In Chile I met Graciela Mandijano, who had spent a year or more in New York, living in the settlement house connected with the Spring Street Presbyterian Church. She was lyrical in her description of the experience. "It was in New York that I found myself. In Chile people had come to see me because I was somebody's daughter or niece or cousin. In New York they came to see me, not because of my connections, but because I was I!" She had been received as an individual, and there was no doubt as to her attitude toward our country.

The Spanish-speaking students in this country below the university level often attend Roman Catholic schools; graduates favor our technical and professional schools rather than the liberal arts departments of the universities. Both of these circumstances make it difficult for them to come into contact with the Protestant churches and the more characteristic aspects in American life. However, we have met Spanish-speaking students in the home of a local pastor. They are delightful to have about. Their great need is hospitality and personal friendliness. Great is our reward when we extend it to them.

Spanish American Baptist Seminary, Los Angeles

This divinity student is representative of scores of Spanish young men who are training for the Christian ministry.

) CHAPTER 9 (

What Shall We Do?

WE HAVE endeavored to portray the vast panorama of the life of the Spanish-speaking people of our country from the hidden valleys of New Mexico to the enforced intimacies of the New York subway. Now we come to the questions: What difference should these people make to us? What can we do as Christians, as Protestants, as church members, to include them more fully in the richer aspects of American life?

We can help to rid ourselves and others of several commonly accepted stereotypes concerning Spanish-speaking Americans.

Once I tried to tell a group of Y.M.C.A. boys in Nebraska about Latin American attitudes toward life, but I could not get them beyond the idea that every Mexican has a knife concealed upon his person that he is most anxious to plunge into somebody's back. On the evidence of movies, pulp magazines, and comic books the boys were sure that I was wrong and that they were right. It did no good to tell them that I had traveled in many parts of Mexico, at all hours, and usually alone, and that I have never had the least occasion to be afraid. Their picture could not be changed by my testimony. I fear that there are many like them. Actually, except in times of revolution, Mexico is a peaceful place. The chief knives carried by Mexicans are big *machetes*, manufactured in Connecticut, which are most useful for harvesting crops or in cutting one's way through underbrush and which are certainly not in the concealed weapons classification. The Mexican workers in this country have a remarkable reputation for harmlessness. It is time that our story writers cast them in another and more truthful role.

Many people assume that Mexicans in the United States are lazy. Their chief evidence seems to be pictures of men taking noonday naps. For the climate of Mexico the noonday siesta is probably a good idea, and one of the virtues of the Mexican people that we might well emulate is their ability to relax. But when it comes to work, real work, hard, exhausting work, we are the lazy ones and not the Mexicans. When a Mexican is free from disease, when he has enough food in his stomach to make his body go, and when he is sure that he will be paid, he is a fiend for work. For sheer energy the boys who offer their services to tourists as guides and general helpers are the world's wonder. And their brains are just as active as their hands and feet. They're a nuisance until you hire them; after that they will do anything for you. In this country there are no complaints by employers of slothfulness on the part of Mexican workers. No one who knows them will dub them "lazy."

A persistent libel around New York is that the Puerto Ricans fly in from Puerto Rico only to get on relief. Actually Puerto Ricans have a fear of both government officials and welfare workers that discourages them from seeking assistance from these sources. As the last to be hired they are commonly the first to be fired, which means that their employment follows the minor fluctuations of business. In recent years the proportion of Puerto Ricans on relief has varied from 6 to 10 per cent, and most of these have been mothers with small children who cannot work because they cannot find day care for their children. As with other groups, the number of Puerto Ricans on welfare depends upon business conditions.

Many people assume that the only people who are really clean are those who have white skins and that therefore the large number of Spanish-speaking Americans whose skins are darker must be dirty. Actually the cleanliness of a people largely depends upon the climate and the availability of bathing facilities. In the tropics water is usually abundant and bathing a pleasant experience. Employers testify to the exceptional cleanliness of the Puerto Ricans.

The background of the Mexicans is quite different. The interior of Mexico is high, cold, and singularly destitute of rivers, while such as do exist only run part of the time. The areas to which they have come in the United States are quite similar. According to the boast of a southern Californian, their rivers are so smart that they get their work done in three months out of the year and stand by in a fine state of emptiness the rest of the time. When one considers that Mexicans quite literally do the dirty work wherever they are, and that water is usually difficult to come by, the degree of cleanliness to which they commonly attain is to be wondered at. Yet from all sorts of hovels, shacks, and tenements, Mexican young people manage to emerge all spick and span, in well pressed and immaculate clothes. The price that they must pay in effort for personal cleanliness is often high, and yet they manage to meet it. For this they deserve far more honor than they commonly receive.

All that any group of people can ask is to be judged on a retail rather than a wholesale basis. Instead of being plastered with a label because of their language or their complexion, they ask for an individual appraisal. It can be pointed out that there are shiftless and dirty Anglo-Americans, but we would not think it fair for our nation to be judged by them. All that other peoples can ask is the courtesy of a similar discrimination.

To approach Spanish-speaking Americans sympathetically we need a finer appreciation of their background.

Behind the Spanish-speaking people of our country lies a great artistic tradition, and one that is surprisingly accessible to us. On the Spanish side, the Sorolla Room in the Hispanic Museum in New York city is one of the most thrilling spots in this country. The eye is overwhelmed by the brilliance of the color and the seeming liveliness of the movement. Spain becomes a flashing reality. On the Indian side, the work of Rivera and Orozco may be seen in the Detroit Art Museum, at Dartmouth College, and in the New School of Social Research in New York. Modern Mexico has given American art its most recent and arresting inspiration.

As thousands of American women and some men have discovered, Mexico is a shoppers' paradise. For this there are three reasons. The products on sale are always interesting and often beautiful, and the range is wide: art work, blankets, leatherwork, glassware, pottery, jewelry. Each object is a new creation and neither matches nor "nests" with anything else. It is fun buying them; salesmanship in Mexico is a form of sport. The price is usually low, particularly if one penetrates below the border.

Mexican products are quite generally available in the United States. We once acquired what we thought was a good set of blue glass in a factory in Guadalajara for only $3.50 our money. As breakage has cut down the set and as we have desired to expand it we have picked up additional pieces from the same factory, but for a much higher price, in all sorts of places in this country. There are also stores that handle only Mexican handiwork.

Mexicans and Puerto Ricans are primarily people with the same hopes and fears as the rest of us. They are just as much the children of God as are we. Our duty and our opportunity is to accept them as such. All they ask is that they be accepted as individuals on the basis of their individual worth, rather than being classified as members of a peculiar group on the basis of fanciful misconceptions. To think in terms of the members of a crowd rather than of the crowd as a whole is not easy, but it is always the Christian thing to do. In the case of Spanish-speaking Americans, there are many barriers to acquaintance and understanding—language, occupation, place of residence.

The easiest contacts are through educational institutions. We visited one of the state supported colleges of Texas where the dean claimed that there were no distinctions between young people of Spanish-speaking ancestry and Anglos, and we were told by a faculty member that pressure was being put on the sororities to persuade them to pledge at least one girl for each chapter from the Mexican students. We suspect that some of this was window dressing in response to pressures that have been put upon the school, but it was wholesome even to have the issue raised.

A special program of service to foreign students, including those of Spanish-speaking background, is offered by the Committee on Friendly Relations among Foreign Students. It was founded to study the needs of these students, to expand the opportunities open to them, and to stimulate communities to share in the experience of international relations. Many individuals and private organizations, such as church boards, the Ford Foundation, the Y. M. and Y. W. C. A., are giving their support to the committee.

The committee's program is varied. The Port of Entry Services

are particularly significant. "Foreign Student Advisers," wearing blue armbands so that they may easily be spotted, meet the ships and planes of incoming students. The bewildered newcomers are helped to get through the multitudinous details of their entry with the least possible embarrassment and stress.

Throughout the year the committee helps and advises with the institution of campus and community programs designed to help integrate the students into their environment and to acquaint others with the rich contributions they can make to campus and community life. Counseling, information, and program services are included in the plan to promote mutual understanding and appreciation.

The committee has definite suggestions for church groups, other organizations, and individuals who sincerely want to extend the hand of friendship to these students. Most of the suggestions are based on two principles: take an intelligent interest in the student as a human being, trying to understand his thoughts and feelings; share your own everyday interests with him in a simple, natural way. Churches are cautioned not to regard these students simply as resource speakers to be whisked into a meeting to fill a place on the program and promptly forgotten when it is over.

Possibly the staff would consider the following statement by a student from Paraguay as representing one fine initial approach to friendship with foreign students:

"I cannot forget K. K., a boy with whom I got so well acquainted as to consider him my brother, and I know he feels the same about me. He took me home for Christmas, giving me a wonderful chance to see life in a small community and a typical farm family. He helped me in everything I needed and was so eager to learn about my country that right now he knows just about as much as I do."[1]

Two Spanish-speaking students were invited into a church home in New Jersey, after having met the family through a church group meeting. The several small children in the home were delighted with their visitors and asked them innumerable questions. The students seemed to respond with pleasure and soon were asking questions themselves, about the garden, the hobby room, and at last—timidly—about the recipes the hostess had used in preparing the meal. Before they left, the students had promised to come back and cook a genuine Spanish meal as a special treat for the children!

If you live in a college or university community, it is a simple matter to find out if there are students of Spanish-speaking American background or from Latin American countries, and then to include them in

[1] *The Unofficial Ambassadors,* Report of the Committee on Friendly Relations among Foreign Students, 1952, p. 3.

church or personal social occasions. They are likely to be most attractive, as the Spanish tradition stresses the social graces. To arrive in an institution of higher learning is also evidence of either unusual ability or ambition. Students of Spanish-speaking antecedents are not just ordinary young people. They are interesting to meet and well worth knowing.

Probably the most natural relations between Anglos and Spanish-speaking Americans are to be found in the high schools of the Southwest. Here day-by-day contacts lay the basis for real friendships. The home can encourage or discourage such relationships. The church can promote them. To do so is to be fair with young people who face rather more difficulties than the average and at the same time to strengthen the unity of our nation.

Perhaps the most discouraging discovery in connection with the preparation of this book has been the obliviousness of many of our communities to the very existence of the Mexican in their midst. In the sugar beet country the people who attend Protestant churches may have seen the Mexicans about, but they regard them as part of the scenery rather than as human beings. Even the ministers appear to have no contacts whatever with them.

We hope that this book will inspire some of its readers to take thought for their forgotten neighbors, at least to the point of being conscious of their existence. As is usually the case, the best contacts are through the children. If there is a migrant center maintained by the state council of churches or by the National Council of Churches in your vicinity, your Sunday school class or young people's group would undoubtedly enjoy visiting it, and perhaps playing with the young people whom it found there. If you are conducting a vacation church school and there are Mexican children about, why not invite them to participate?

The Puerto Ricans are our newest comers, and offer an unusual opportunity. Outside of New York city, their movements are being directed to a considerable degree by the Government of Puerto Rico, largely on a group basis. If a group of Puerto Ricans should come to your town or city it is because some industry asked for them, the state employment office was convinced that they were needed, and the Government of Puerto Rico has approved of their coming. This is far different from the haphazard, unguided migrations of the past. The Puerto Ricans are American citizens. The community is in some measure responsible for their coming. This being so, it would be a lovely and most American gesture for the churches to make them welcome. They are strangers in a strange land; they need help in all sorts of adjustments, but most of all they need a sense of belonging. Here is a chance for some inspired Christian helpfulness.

No one who has come to know our Spanish-speaking Americans has failed to like them. They are a friendly, cordial people, with rather more and better manners than the rest of us. They have much to add to our American life not only through their physical vigor but through their feeling for the beautiful and the liveliness of their imaginations. They have an excellent capacity for religious understanding and expression. They can bring a new vigor to our churches. It should be our ambition to include them more fully in both our community and our church life.

A Short Reading List

The purpose of this list is to suggest recent and available books to provide background for the study of Americans of Spanish heritage. The views expressed in the several books are not necessarily in harmony with those of the author and the publishers of this volume.

Leaders of groups using *Within These Borders* as a text for study and action may secure supplementary material by applying to their own denominational literature headquarters. From these sources and from book stores they may order *The Adult Guide on Spanish-speaking Americans,* by Edwin F. Tewksbury. Price 50 cents.

Accent on Liberty, edited by Mabel M. Sheibley. Contains several dramatic stories of Spanish Americans. New York, Friendship Press, 1952. Paper $1.25; cloth $2.00.

American Me, by Beatrice Griffith. Boston, Houghton Mifflin Co., 1948. $3.50.

Beyond Good Friday, by Edith J. Agnew. A one-act play about Spanish-speaking Americans in the Southwest. New York, Friendship Press, 1953. 35 cents.

Forgotten People; a study of New Mexicans, by George Isidore Sánchez. A university professor of Spanish-speaking ancestry analyzes the life of his people. Albuquerque, University of New Mexico Press, 1940. $2.00.

Fun and Festival among America's Peoples, by Katherine Ferris Rohrbough. A treasure house of suggestions for those responsible for planning programs and parties. New York, Friendship Press, 1943. 50 cents.

It Happened in Taos, by Jesse Taylor Reid. The story of a successful social experiment in a Spanish-speaking community in the mountains of New Mexico. Albuquerque, University of New Mexico Press, 1946. $2.50.

Know Your Fellow American Citizen from Puerto Rico, picture pamphlet. An appeal by the Government of Puerto Rico for fair treatment for her citizens as they come to the mainland. The Office of the Government of Puerto Rico, 1026 Seventeenth St., N. W., Washington, D. C., 1952. Free.

Latin Americans in Texas, by Pauline R. Kibbe. How the Government of Texas has endeavored to improve the relations between her Spanish-speaking and her other residents. Albuquerque, University of New Mexico Press, 1946. $3.50.

Migratory Labor in American Agriculture. Report of the President's Commission on Migratory Labor. Washington, D. C., Government Printing Office, 1951. 75 cents.

North from Mexico; the Spanish-speaking people of the United States, by Carey McWilliams. A current report on the status, economic and otherwise, of those of Mexican descent in this country. Philadelphia, J. B. Lippincott Co., 1949. $4.00.

Papi, by Eleanor Hull. New York, Friendship Press, 1953. Paper $1.25; cloth $2.00.

Puerto Rican Journey; New York's newest migrants, by Charles Wright Mills, Clarence Senior, and Rose Kohn Goldsen. The results of a recent study of Puerto Rican immigration to New York. New York, Harper and Brothers, 1950. $3.00.

Southern California Country; an island on the land, by Carey McWilliams. Although this deals with Spanish-speaking Americans only indirectly, it gives an excellent analysis of the forces that have molded Southern California. New York, Duell, Sloan and Pearce, 1946. $3.75.

Strangers—and Neighbors; the story of our Puerto Rican Citizens, by Clarence Senior. A popular interpretation of the Puerto Ricans in our midst. New York, Anti-defamation League of B'nai B'rith, 1953. 25 cents.

The Secret Suitcase, by Dorothy W. Andrews and Louise B. Scott. New York, Friendship Press, 1953. Paper $1.25; cloth $2.00.

Who? Spanish-speaking Americans in the U. S. A., edited by Mae Hurley Ashworth. New York, Friendship Press, 1953. 50 cents.

THE AUTHOR

JOHN R. SCOTFORD was born and raised in Chicago and received his education first at Dartmouth College and later at Union Theological Seminary. After holding several Congregational pastorates in Texas, Oklahoma, and Ohio, he joined the staff of the *Missionary Herald,* where he took on a great many assignments involving extended travel. During those years he became more and more familiar with the status and problems of Spanish-speaking Americans in the U.S.A., an area of knowledge he had been exploring since his early pastorates in the Southwest.

After twelve years with the *Missionary Herald* he was invited to the editorship of *Advance,* a post he occupied until 1950. During the past three years, in addition to writing many articles, he has traveled even more extensively through areas in which Spanish-speaking Americans are concentrated, investigating closely, and in person, many Mexican settlements in this country, as well as a great many communities in which Puerto Ricans, Cubans, and others, have largely located.

Dr. Scotford has written several books and pictorial presentations, including *Spanning a Continent, Together We Build America,* and *The Church Beautiful.* In addition to his journalistic activities, he is also a well-known figure in the field of church architecture, and is today a member of the board of managers of the Bureau of Church Building of the National Council of Churches.

THE FORMAT

The text of this book is set in Caledonia on the linotype by Ruttle, Shaw & Wetherill, Inc., of Philadelphia, Pennsylvania. It was printed by offset lithography by General Offset Company, Inc., of New York. It was bound in paper by F. M. Charlton Company, Inc., and in cloth by Charles H. Bohn and Company, both of New York.

Typographic design by Patricia Birdwood
Jacket and paper cover designed by Rafael Palacios
Binding by Louise E. Jefferson